Creative Library Marketing
and Publicity

Creative Library Marketing and Publicity

Best Practices

Edited by
Robert J. Lackie
and
M. Sandra Wood

ROWMAN & LITTLEFIELD
Lanham • Boulder • New York • London

Published by Rowman & Littlefield
A wholly owned subsidiary of The Rowman & Littlefield Publishing Group, Inc.
4501 Forbes Boulevard, Suite 200, Lanham, Maryland 20706
www.rowman.com

Unit A, Whitacre Mews, 26-34 Stannary Street, London SE11 4AB

British Library Cataloguing in Publication Information Available

Library of Congress Cataloging-in-Publication Data

Creative library marketing and publicity : best practices / Robert J. Lackie, M. Sandra Wood.
pages cm. — (Best practices in library services)
Includes bibliographical references and index.
ISBN 978-1-4422-5420-6 (hardcover : alk. paper) — ISBN 978-1-4422-5421-3 (pbk. : alk. paper) — ISBN 978-1-4422-5422-0 (ebook)
1. Libraries—Marketing. 2. Libraries—Public relations. 3. Libraries—United States—Case studies. I. Lackie, Robert J., 1966–, editor. II. Wood, M. Sandra, editor.
Z716.3.C78 2015
021.7—dc23
2015015115

Printed in the United States of America

In memory of Michael Scott Wood,
June 1, 1989–February 19, 2015

Contents

Preface

When speaking with any library professional about the importance of public awareness in regard to their library's continued existence, the conversation will inevitably lead to discussions about the necessity of marketing and promoting library resources and services in order to gain important visibility and support. The American Marketing Association (AMA) defines marketing as "the activity, set of institutions, and processes for creating, communicating, delivering, and exchanging offerings that have value for customers, clients, partners, and society at large" (approved July 2013, https://www.ama.org/AboutAMA/Pages/Definition-of-Marketing.aspx). Like many public institutions, all types of libraries—academic, public, and school libraries—relate to the AMA's definition and attempt to promote themselves and their services and programs in various ways, with many developing authentic marketing plans and successful promotional tools to establish and build positive relationships with their various constituents. And in fact, by effectively incorporating innovative and creative marketing, promotional, publicity, and advocacy efforts, whether through traditional or nontraditional methods, ideas, and campaigns, many libraries have improved their reputations as dynamic, inviting institutions and gained important, continuing (loyal) support.

Obviously, marketing has a significant impact on and can even positively change how the community perceives a library and all of its resources. Conversely, libraries who do not proactively promote themselves and their resources and services to their users and supporters face the very real risk of losing their users and support—and maybe even eventually closing their doors. However, even though library personnel are being charged with creating marketing and promotions plans and getting buy-in from their constituents, most library professionals and paraprofessionals do not have the education or experience needed—and marketing is probably not high on the list of priorities within their normal job descriptions. Many academic, public, and school library professionals are genuinely at a loss when they are suddenly tasked with dealing with vital promotion, publicity, branding, and advocacy priorities—all important aspects of marketing their libraries.

Creative Library Marketing and Publicity: Best Practices focuses on some of these most visible aspects of marketing for libraries—promotion, publicity, branding, and advocacy. Drawing on the best practices, experience, and expertise of library personnel from public, academic, and school libraries, this volume brings together a variety of marketing plans and creative methods for promoting libraries and their programs and services to a twenty-first-century audience. All library employees should be able to take away something from these creative, successful efforts and be able to apply tips, techniques, and best-practice suggestions to their own library marketing efforts.

HOW THE BOOK IS ORGANIZED

Creative Library Marketing and Publicity: Best Practices is an edited book of twelve chapters, with authors drawn from small to large public, academic, and school libraries, systems, and organizations. Each chapter describes a library's successful experience with marketing, branding, or promoting a library service or program, providing information about planning, actual promotion techniques, and evaluating the success of the plan or promotion methods utilized. Most importantly, chapter authors include tips and best practices for readers. Many of these ideas and techniques are applicable across the board, so the chapters within this volume will help you implement similar methods to promote your library services and programs and spark different and unique uses for these techniques.

In chapter 1, "Building a Foundation for Marketing Success," Jeannie Allen, at Kitsap Regional Library in Washington, discusses in detail the research process and questions every library professional should answer in order to develop solid marketing goals that will help gain a deeper understanding of the needs of any library organization and the unique community it serves. Instead of diving into somewhat clever campaigns that only gain the library a headline or two, she instead walks us through the process of developing a marketing plan that will do much more than just promote a product or service, but one that will build awareness of the library in a way that no single approach can.

In order to build faculty awareness, interest, and engagement in open access publishing, supporting their university's newly adopted Open Access Policy, in chapter 2, "Conversations: Building Relationships and Using Constituent Voice in Outreach," Letha Kay Goger discusses how the University of California, Merced Library enlisted faculty voices for a video campaign designed to address issues of promise and concern around publishing with an open access model. This chapter details the library's outreach and promotion campaign, including steps taken to engage faculty, dissemination, community response, and suggestions for building a similar library campaign.

Brent Bloechle discusses in chapter 3, "Plano Public Library System: Building a Social Media Presence," how PPLS in Texas began with one blog in 2008, but as patrons migrated to new social media platforms, it followed along to meet their specific needs, such as creating the *Job Center* blog during the economic downturn. Details on how PPLS built and maintains a successful social media program that currently includes active participation on six blogs and seven social media sites, including Instagram, are provided. Strategies for staffing and maintaining the levels of support necessary for this broad social media presence, as well as guidelines for posting and recommendations for content, are also included in this chapter.

In chapter 4, "Creating Campus Buzz with Promotional Videos," the team of Heather A. Dalal, Paris Hannon, and Robert J. Lackie at Rider University Libraries in New Jersey describes in detail the creation, promotion, and initial reception of the Guardians of the Library promotional video series based on a popular culture reference—Marvel's blockbuster movie *Guardians of the Galaxy*—and how this newest series concerning library tools and services was marketed for increased visibility at Rider University Libraries in New Jersey. This chapter also includes advice and best practices for other librarians wishing to successfully create and market promotional videos.

The team of Mary E. Edwards, Hannah F. Norton, Michele R. Tennant, Nina C. Stoyan-Rosenzweig, and Matthew Daley, in chapter 5, "Promotion, Publicity, and Beyond: Using a Marketing Plan and Innovative Strategies to Reach Users in an Academic Health Science Center Library," describes successful efforts to promote library services and activities, including how they identified the need for and drafted a flexible plan for advertising to the University of Florida Health Science Center Library community and beyond. The chapter also expands on innovative ways their library marketing plan was implemented and promoted, concluding with the lessons and best practices learned about marketing and publicity.

Jessica Ford and Jim Staley at Mid-Continent Public Library in Missouri detail their successful branding efforts in chapter 6, "Branding for Relevance: A Public Library's Continuing Campaign for Access." They set out to rebrand around a concept that encompassed what libraries are truly about—access—which became the basis for the library's mission statement, strategic plan, employee resources planning, and building design, as well as the animating idea for advertising, social media, and public relations campaigns that followed. This chapter lays out the original thinking, and how the branding and marketing message has been used, adapted, and bolstered since the initial rollout.

In chapter 7, "People Do Still Read E-mail! E-mail Marketing as an Academic Library Outreach Tool," Jamie Hazlitt at the William H. Hannon Library of Loyola Marymount University in California discusses how libraries can leverage e-mail marketing and communicate their brand to their customers. In this chapter, readers will learn about decisions made before publishing the first issue of their monthly e-newsletter *Happenings @ Hannon*; how LMU librarians developed and continue to grow the mailing list; resources and workflows needed to publish regularly; and how the impact of *Happenings* is assessed at LMU. Integrated throughout are suggestions and best practices for librarians considering launching their own periodical e-newsletter.

Erica Thorsen discusses in chapter 8, "Increasing Library Use: It's a Long Story," how the librarians at Albemarle High School Library in Virginia have revolutionized aspects of their library, moving it from a traditional library to a post-Gutenberg learning and resource space, where students can access a wide variety of resources ranging from devices and databases to makerspaces and a music lab. This chapter also provides recommended best practices for others interested in promoting and publicizing their own library, especially regarding space renovations, updating the collection, and capitalizing on Web presence and social media.

Coleen Meyers-Martin and Lynn D. Lampert, at California State University, Northridge's Oviatt Library, describe in chapter 9, "If You Build It, Will They Come? Marketing a New Library Space," their library's eight-month, multifaceted communications and marketing campaign, which promoted a two-and-a-half-million-dollar renovation of a new Learning Commons. Details such as staffing, funding, and the time involved to coordinate a two-phase marketing campaign provide insight into the many logistical details of managing a grand-scale project, as well as discuss best project management practices, enabling the chapter to be referenced as a how-to manual for promoting and marketing new library spaces.

Chapter 10, "Marketing on a Shoestring: Publicity and Promotion in a Small Public Library," by Heather Nicholson, formerly at Coaldale Public Library in Alberta, Canada, argues that even without the advantages of a large budget or dedicated professionally trained communications staff, it is possible to conduct effective marketing to communicate with stakeholders, remain relevant, and provide high-quality programs and services. In this chapter, Nicholson shares general strategies that can be applied to almost any small library, including strategic planning, branding or visual identity, programmatic evaluation, stretching yourself, using social media, networking, and looking to the future.

Library programming is an essential part of outreach, allowing librarians to become the face of their library and promote their services. In chapter 11, "Library Programming: Methods for Creation, Collaboration, Delivery, and Outreach," Amanda Piekart and Bonnie Lafazan of Berkeley College Library (campuses in New York and New Jersey) provide the tools for developing relationships and collaboration beyond the library and increasing campus community participation when it comes to library programming promotion and outreach. They also explain how to reach diverse populations using an array of delivery methods and provide a variety of program ideas, as well as concrete examples of how to create meaningful, successful programming events.

"'Flipping the Switch' for School Library Advocacy" is the final chapter in this volume, by noted school librarian and nationally known expert speaker, consultant, and advocate for school librarianship Sara Kelly Johns. She talks about the evolution of the role of school librarians to include increased emphasis and commitment to leadership and program and legislative advocacy. In this chapter, Johns emphasizes building a personal core of advocates/ champions through the development of a strong, active, and targeted marketing plan, which she details. To assist librarians to become aware and active leaders for advocacy, she also provides key messaging and advice from experts in the field, as well as a wealth of resources to help lead librarians through the Promotion + Marketing = Advocates process.

From the traditional to new and creative marketing and promotional methods and plans; from small libraries to large libraries; from academic to public to school libraries, systems, and organizations—*Creative Library Marketing and Publicity: Best Practices* offers expert and accomplished plans, tips, and suggestions, and plenty of best practices to all types of information professionals so that they can adapt and use them successfully at their own libraries in pursuit of their own successful, targeted marketing and promotional efforts.

Chapter One

Building a Foundation for Marketing Success

Jeannie Allen — Kitsap Regional Library

When I tell people I market libraries for a living, it is often met with a declaration: "I didn't know you could market a library?" Or with a sense of confusion: "Why does a library need a marketer?" Why indeed? Everybody loves the library, right? At this point in the conversation, I do a little spontaneous market research and ask the question: "What purpose does the library serve in your community?" A library enthusiast will wax nostalgic, weaving a tale of libraries of their past or bypass the library completely and talk of their love of books. They may answer with a tale of reverence, and an appreciation for an institution that guards knowledge and history, speaking of the library as more of an archive than an active, essential foundation for a thriving community. I am also all too familiar with the more dreaded responses: "Libraries are irrelevant." "I read on my tablet." Or, my favorite, "Why do we need libraries when we have Google?"

Of course, the millions of people who use a library every day know its value, but even many them do not understand everything the library does. When libraries are funded by their communities and every dollar is being stretched to provide the best possible service, is it responsible to put funds and other valuable resources into marketing? Absolutely. Libraries are changing as quickly as the world is; it would be irresponsible not to.

Somewhere along the way the message of why libraries exist fell away, and libraries let the message of what they are become about a product: books. The tools libraries use to serve their communities are varied and change more rapidly than they have been able to communicate. As a result, our communities are losing touch with the true value of the library. Libraries are not now—nor have they ever been—about a product, the buildings, or even the librarian. If libraries continue to communicate their value as a product to be offered, they will fail. Technology is rapidly changing. The moment you succeed in connecting the public to a message about the next big thing the library has embraced, it slips away and becomes something else.

Who knows a good story better than the library? It is time to tell the library's story. What do libraries stand for? In order to deliver a powerful message that connects to the emotional core of why libraries are and will always be essential, we need to understand better than anyone why we do what we do. It is our responsibility to make sure the people who invest in libraries for the future of their communities see the value in their investment.

In the beginning of 2012, Kitsap Regional Library, which serves the residents of Kitsap County, Washington, did not have a marketing department. I was hired as the library's first marketing manager, with the task of developing an idea of what it means to market a library from scratch. The library had some large, overarching goals to accomplish, and the organization was progressive enough to understand it needed help with a game plan. If you go into any library today, whether it has a formal marketing department or not, you will find some level of marketing in place. Librarians, PR staff, and others bravely step into the role of marketer and do the best they can to communicate all that their library has to offer. Kitsap Regional Library was no exception. For many years, the programming staff and the PR department had worked together and been successful in creating a certain level of awareness for the products and programs the library had to offer. But marketing a library is about more than building awareness for an individual product or service. It is about how the community, patrons, non-users, leaders, stakeholders, children, grandparents, teachers, businesses, voters, and taxpayers all view the role of the library. To market a library, and not just the products it provides, you must analyze all of the current efforts and possibilities and create a plan to direct those efforts to accomplish the larger goals. To do this, you have to look at the efforts as part of the whole and create a foundation for marketing that can generate support far into the future.

How do you set marketing goals for a library? In business, the goal is easy: make more money, but when you are marketing a library, the goals are not so clear. A solid foundation for marketing can only come from research and a well-crafted marketing plan.

This chapter will discuss some of the challenges that arise when building a marketing plan and setting some initial marketing goals, as well as provide some possible solutions. Some best practices for building a strong marketing foundation will also be highlighted. In a lot of ways, Kitsap Regional Library is still in the research phases of building a strong foundation for our marketing, yet it has already experienced some great successes, indicators that the library is on the right track. The marketing plan developed has helped shape very clear goals based on a solid understanding of why we do what we do. A marketing plan may not be as sexy as a grassroots, guerilla marketing effort that goes viral on YouTube, and it probably will not get you recognized in the next issue of *Library Journal*, but it is the first step to building a campaign that will get you long-term results.

PLAN TO PLAN

The research that a marketing plan is built on is absolutely essential. While conducting the research, keep these questions in mind:

- What is the current state of the organization?
- Why does the library do what it does?
- How does the library do it?
- What is the current marketing situation?
- How do the patrons currently use the library?
- What is the current perception/idea of the library's role in the community?
- What is the makeup of the community?
- What are the community goals?
- Who is the target audience?
- What is happening nationally in the library industry?
- How does the library want to evolve?

When these questions can be answered with clarity, then you will probably find you have gathered everything you need to create the plan. You may find during the research process, as Kitsap Regional Library did, that answering some of these questions becomes the first goal of the plan.

WHAT IS THE CURRENT MARKETING SITUATION?

Brand Audit

The research that goes into understanding the organization's existing marketing is 90 percent of the work. Do it right and the marketing plan may just write itself. The best place to start is with a complete audit of the library's brand.

If done right, a brand audit will give you insight into every aspect of the organization. To avoid a rookie mistake—the need to return again and again for missed information—make sure you have a full understanding of what information needs to be collected and how it will be documented before starting.

So what do you look for in a brand audit? Every point where an organization's brand intersects with people creates an idea of who that organization is. Every interaction is an opportunity to strengthen or weaken that relationship. Take a look at how the organization is seen not only from the patron's perspective, but also from the perspective of staff, stakeholders, and non-users.

To start forming an idea of what the brand is currently communicating, review all of the following:

- Any current planning documents, such as a strategic plan, social media plan, director's goals, etc.
- Annual reports—for the past three years
- Statistical information—for the past three years
- Press releases—for the past three years
- Marketing information—advertising and communications for the past three years
- Physical and virtual locations

What to Identify

Reviewing all of these pieces will give you a clear picture of the marketing situation and where the work will need to begin. In the physical spaces, do a walk-through to understand what is communicated by the first impressions of the spaces, layout, signage, and presentation of staff and products. Pay close attention to the look. Is there consistency? Do the materials, spaces, and people communicate the message you want them to communicate? How do they make you feel? Are they communicating in a way that connects strongest to a target market group?

While reviewing these materials, a clear picture of the state of the organization should start to take shape. Take the structure of the marketing plan (outlined further on in this chapter) and start filling it in with the information on hand. Where are the gaps? Surveys, focus groups, and conversations with leadership, staff, and community will complete the picture.

You may find that the most effective use of marketing efforts will begin with addressing the spaces and staff. Before pushing a message out into the community, make sure the experience the customer receives matches the message and the promise you want the marketing to convey.

One of the first steps in developing the goals of a marketing plan is to fully understand how the key leaders in the organization view the role of the library in the community. To start this process, schedule one-on-one meetings with key leaders and stakeholders and ask the following questions:

- What is it that the library does?
- Who does the library do this for, who is the target customer?
- How does the library do it?

- Why does the library serve customers the way that it does?
- What value do libraries bring to the community, and how are they unique?
- If you could define this library in just one word, what would it be?

These questions are the same questions any organization would answer in the process of developing a mission statement. Your goal should be to hear how each member of your leadership team would answer these questions if they were talking to any member of the community. How aligned is the leadership of the organization in their thinking about the goals and mission? E-mail the questions to each participant a few days before meeting with them, giving them time to consider how they will answer. The meetings should be done one-on-one to give you the opportunity to hear how different the responses can be from one person to the next, without influence from other members of the leadership team. These are the people that are leading the messaging for the entire organization. What kind of picture does each person's answers paint of the organization? Is there consistency in the message from one person to the next? Can they articulate why the library does what it does, or do their answers revolve around the products the library offers, never really connecting to the organization's values and the emotional reasons behind why? Consider this the baseline for the work that needs to be done. A community cannot truly understand what the library offers until the leadership and staff are united in their message. If you have done your job well in marketing, when the staff are in the community, you will hear a consistent message that strikes a chord with your community's values.

WRITE THE PLAN

A marketing plan is a living document. If it is done right, you will be continually executing the plans you have drafted, checking your results, and updating your document to reflect your current position. In Kitsap Regional Library's plan, the goals have been staged for the next two years. The time period of any plan may vary depending on the strength of the organization's current marketing and the complexity of the goals that are developed. When it is complete, it will be one of the most well-rounded accounts of the state of the organization, and it will not only inform marketing decisions, but it will become a quick go-to guide for information when developing everything from press releases and grants to the next strategic plan.

It is always helpful to review the marketing plans of other organizations when creating one. Don't limit yourself to the library industry in your research. These plans give you a starting point, a way to identify what works for you, and what you may want to do differently. The Kitsap Regional Library plan was structured as follows:

- Section 1: Mission, Values, and Unique Selling Proposition
- Section 2: Overview
- Section 3: Marketing Mix
- Section 4: Marketing Strategy
- Section 5: Evaluation
- Section 6: Budget

Section 1: Mission, Values, and Unique Selling Proposition

In this first section, outline the organization's mission, values, and unique selling proposition. This section forms the basis for all of the sections to follow in the marketing plan.

Mission

A mission statement should explain why the organization exists. It should resonate and inspire. A well-written mission is short, easy to remember, and should serve as a guide for setting focused goals.

Values

The values should be reflective of the principles of the organization and the community it serves. They should be simple and direct, and your staff should see themselves represented in them. A great company to look to for developing your organization's values is Zappos. CEO Tony Hseih's book *Delivering Happiness: A Path to Profits, Passion, and Purpose* is a quick read and an invaluable resource if you want to learn more about the impact of values on company culture and how to develop meaningful values for your organization.

Unique Selling Proposition

The term *unique selling proposition* (USP) has grown to mean a number of things in marketing. To many people, it represents what makes an organization different from any other; to others it represents what an organization stands for. For many organizations, this is represented by their tagline. There is debate as to whether taglines in marketing are still useful or relevant. No matter where your opinion falls, it is still crucial to know what makes the organization stand out from the rest and be able to distill it down to the simplest terms, creating the strongest possible message.

During the research process to develop its first marketing plan, Kitsap Regional Library realized that its mission, values, and USP did not communicate what it wanted. These statements should be active tools that are used to motivate, inspire, and drive the organization forward. For many companies, the mission and values are just words living in a document somewhere, never to be thought of again after they are written. In writing Kitsap Regional Library's marketing plan, it was decided to complete it with the preexisting mission, values, and USP in place, knowing that reenvisioning them would be one of the first goals of the plan.

Section 2: Overview

In the overview, develop an introduction that creates an understanding of the organization; this will become an easily accessible place to return to when you need access to key information. Here is a list of some of the things that Kitsap Regional Library included in the introduction to its marketing plan:

- Demographics: Number of people served, summary of the makeup of your population, percentage of population that are cardholders, and percentage of cardholders that have been active in the last year
- Summary of products and services (in the Marketing Mix section below, include a full, detailed outline of every product and service offered)
- Circulation statistics of the virtual and physical collections
- Door counts
- Website views
- Public computer usage
- Collection summary
- Summary of programming

Current Marketing Situation

The second part of the overview is the current marketing situation. Here, outline what plans are currently in place for marketing the organization, and reference any research and documents that were used to build the marketing strategy (Section 4). A complete list of these research points makes it easy to return to them in the future. Some points of reference for the marketing plan might include an ongoing strategic plan, director's goals, studies conducted by the organization or an outside consultant, statistical reports, annual reports, and previous marketing plans. In this section, it may also be helpful to give a detailed report of competitors and allies and create a strength, weakness, opportunity, and threat (SWOT) analysis for the organization (discussed later in this section).

Competitors

It is a common view among many in the library world that libraries do not have competitors. This is simply not true. While libraries do not compete for commerce, they do compete for the attention and financial support of the community. Patrons want to get what they need, when they need it, from the best source possible. Libraries have to continuously create the perception that they are that source. When looking at competitors, note any business (physical or virtual) that offers similar products or services. It is also useful to have a comprehensive list of these organizations and businesses so that you can keep an eye on how they grow and change, allowing you to adjust your marketing strategy to stay competitive.

Allies

Allies are those people and organizations that support the library with dollars, time, and marketing exposure to audiences that they have access to. There are three sections of allies in Kitsap Regional Library's report:

Library. Friends groups, foundation, volunteers, and boards

Media. Local media partners, including print publications, radio, and television

Business and community. Community partners, schools, government, chambers, community service groups, and local businesses

As a side note, one of the goals of Kitsap Regional Library's marketing plan is to create an organized way of managing these partnerships. A partnership is formed between the librarians, branch managers, and leadership of the library and the people within these groups. It is an investment on the library's part when staff go out into the community to build these relationships. The goal should be to make sure the library owns these partnerships. If all of these partnerships are managed in a central place, like a contact management system, it is easier to create a strategy to build and strengthen those connections and make sure no opportunities are missed. It allows the ability to turn those records over to others to manage as change naturally happens; new people in the organization can hit the ground running. Another advantage to this strategy is that it creates a centralized place for this information and the ability to create messaging targeted to these groups.

SWOT

In a traditional strength, weakness, opportunity, and threat (SWOT) analysis, the strengths and weaknesses focus on the internal side of the organization, whereas the opportunities and threats focus externally. Kitsap Regional Library's SWOT analysis developed out of multiple conversations with various levels of organizational leadership. The library looked at its technological capabilities and limitations, current relationships and partnerships, demographics, the capabilities of the staff and spaces, and the current position of the library industry; then, the staff had a series of discussions on those topics. In developing this section of the plan, the need for a fifth section emerged, internal opportunity (SWOTI). This added section identifies opportunities to better support library staff, which will allow the library to build a culture where the staff is eager to communicate to patrons and friends the value of the library.

Section 3: Marketing Mix

In commercial terms, the marketing mix is about finding the right combination of price, products, promotion, and place to create the best income potential. In libraries, a detailed understanding of these factors can help create a better picture of the tools available and how to best use them.

Price

In a business-focused marketing plan, you would answer the question: What is the cost of a product or service? The section would explore the actual cost of each product or service and outline what can reasonably be charged for each.

So how do you develop a price strategy for a library? Too often, in libraries, there is the thought that the products and services are free. This really undervalues what libraries do, not only in the eyes of the community but to the staff as well. A clearly outlined pricing section will communicate the real value of each product and service.

Start with a detailed description of how the organization is funded, including funds received from outside organizations such as friends, foundations, and grants, and the cost of the products and services offered. Then calculate the cost of what the library has to offer, factoring in actual costs of materials, staff time, and marketing. What the library spends each year should balance with the cost of the products and services.

When you calculate price, you will begin to see the true cost of each product and service the library has to offer. What is the opportunity cost of each? By choosing to focus money and time into one area, the library loses the opportunity to do so elsewhere. A price analysis gives your organization a way to take a look at each product and service from a value perspective. It will soon become clear which opportunities should be expanded and which may be draining valuable resources.

Products

In this category, list all of the organization's products and services. Include programming, classes, and initiatives. Because there is a wide range of ways to serve the community, it may be helpful to divide this section into the following:

Products. Physical items including books, DVDs, booklists, audiobooks, etc.

Services. Outreach, bookmobile, readers advisory, etc.

Virtual. Ask-a-Librarian, eCards, databases, etc.

Core events. Industry and community events the library participates in, such as Library Card Signup Month or the local fair

Core classes and groups, adult. Adult programming, book groups, etc.

Core classes and groups, kids and teens. Children's programming, clubs, and groups

Special collections. Collections focused on unique attributes of the community

Programs. Special organizational programs such as One Book, One Community and Summer Reading

Promotion

Most organizations are using any number of print or virtual media to deliver their message. In this section, create a detailed account of every way the organization is communicating its message, as well as the opportunities that are available that could be further explored. Kitsap Regional Library's plan consisted of print, community, online, and human resource categories, and each of these were divided even further into current marketing efforts and areas to explore.

Print

In this section, list every print opportunity the organization is using or would like to explore. Flyers, logo merchandise, and stationery all belong in this section. Some areas to explore might be print advertising or mail opportunities.

In the Community

Where is the organization taking advantage of being visible in the community? This can be guerilla marketing tactics, a bookmobile, word of mouth, media releases, or even going door-to-door. What are you doing now and what could you be doing?

Online

Where does the organization appear online, and is it taking advantage of every opportunity? The easy answers here are the organization's website, e-mail lists, and any social media platforms you may use. When was the last time you Googled your organization? When you do a search of your website, does the description give you the right idea about what the library offers? Do you have full control of your Yelp listings and other similar site listings? Do you have a complete list of media and local organizations, such as business chambers, and any opportunities they may have for partnering in event calendars and press release opportunities? Explore the organization's virtual presence and look at it from the perspective of a patron.

Human Resources

Every place that information about an organization appears is an opportunity to create a perception of the organization. Although marketing efforts most often target staff and community, it is good to have a say in how the messaging is being crafted for potential hires. In this section, list all of the places the HR team currently recruits; this could be print ads, virtual job boards, universities, state library associations, and national professional organizations such as the American Library Association.

Place

Yet another area where the Kitsap Regional Library felt further division was helpful was that of place, both physical and virtual settings. Physical locations—and any place the organization can be discovered online—belong in this section. The virtual section should include everything from vendor partners and mobile apps to social media accounts.

Marketing Targets

This is an extremely important section of the marketing plan; the research done leading up to this point will have a lot to do with informing this section of the plan. Define the different groups that make up the community and how they interact with the library. While developing its plan, Kitsap Regional Library identified four groups, each with a unique relationship with the library. Through targeted messaging to each of these groups, there is an opportunity to strengthen the overall perception of the library.

- Staff
- Patrons: divided into groups based on how they use the library
- Support: foundation, volunteers, friends groups, donors
- Partnerships: community partners, business community, civic organizations

Working with consulting company OrangeBoy, Kitsap Regional Library conducted an in-depth study of its patron base. Out of that study, the library was able to divide patrons into a number of categories (referred to as clusters) based not on standard demographics, but on the way that they interact with the library. Because of these clusters, Kitsap Regional Library is now able to focus on strengthening its connection to these groups by delivering messaging targeted to their specific needs and interests in the way that they prefer to communicate.

The cliché in marketing is true: if you are trying to market to everyone, you are marketing to no one. Libraries often have a hard time accepting this. Libraries are created to serve everyone, but that does not mean that they should try to market to everyone. The biggest benefit of the process that Kitsap Regional Library went through with OrangeBoy was the larger conversation that was had across the organization about the clusters that developed. How does the library interact differently with each of these groups? Does the library want to encourage one group to transition into another? Based on the priorities of the community served and the short- and long-term goals of the library, which of these groups should be the main focus for marketing efforts? Before priorities are set in a marketing plan, you need to know the answers to all of these questions. Answering these questions in an organizational discussion will go a long way to make sure your marketing efforts are well understood and fully supported.

Through these discussions Kitsap Regional Library was able to determine the priority of its target groups, the highest priority being the library staff. The understanding of what the library does, and why, needs to be clarified at every staffing level. Without working to strengthen and unify these ideas internally, any external marketing effort is doomed to have only limited success. Focusing on your people first is just smart marketing. With the rise of social media and the decline in effectiveness of print and media advertising, the strength of an organization's culture is everything. Marketing to staff is the lowest-cost option for an organization with few dollars to spend on advertising, and it has the highest yield. Creating a workforce that feels supported and has a rich understanding of what the organization is all about, its products and services, and why it is essential to the community builds pride in the work that is being done. A happy employee who understands and believes in what their organization values and stands for is the easiest way to build visibility in the community.

Kitsap Regional Library's second priority was established after two half-day workshops with OrangeBoy and many roundtable discussions. Two clusters were selected for the focus of the external marketing efforts: patrons who use the library primarily to serve children, and patrons who primarily use downloadable collections and digital resources. For the Kitsap Regional Library and community, these priorities made the most sense.

How do you increase awareness of the library in your community and make sure that you are able to deliver on service expectations? If your library system were to get a sudden surge of customers, would your collection and staffing levels be able to deliver your service promise? It is a chicken-and-egg scenario: more satisfied users can lead to better funding and more opportunities for an organization; but until you have the resources to support a larger patron base, you have to move carefully. Kitsap Regional Library has made very good use of limited resources. The choice to focus marketing on the two selected clusters mentioned before was focused on maximizing less utilized products and services and increasing visibility without causing additional stress to staffing and collections. With a fixed budget, staffing cannot simply be increased. Always keep the user experience in mind and think about what might happen if your marketing efforts are very successful. A well-executed marketing plan that does not result in a great user experience can do much more harm than good.

Section 4: Marketing Strategy

This is the fun part of the plan. The research is done, the priorities have been narrowed, and the marketing targets have been identified. Here is where a little creativity can come into play. In this section, main goals are identified, strategies for each goal are created, and specific activities are developed to accomplish each strategy.

Set a number of goals, strategies, and activities that you can accomplish with the resources available in the time period you've set out. Be realistic about what the organization is capable of accomplishing, but make sure to create a vision that inspires you to set and reach your goals.

In the beginning of this section, set the larger, overarching goals, the main objectives. What is the end result your organization is trying to achieve? Within each goal, strategies are identified. These strategies are smaller goals that fit into the overarching goals defined at the beginning. Develop each strategy further by identifying individual activities, the steps you will take to complete each strategy. For the first draft of Kitsap Regional Library's marketing plan the goals were:

- Redefine the library brand
- Develop internal marketing
- Increase visibility and awareness of the library
- Strengthen the relationship between the PR Department and staff

Figure 1.1 shows an example of how this section of the marketing plan might look.

Section 5: Evaluation

In this section, you will identify how to measure whether the goals, strategies, and activities you developed in Section 4 are having the desired impact. This may be a challenge. Depending on how an organization has collected statistical information in the past, it may take some digging to discover who

MARKETING STRATEGY

1. Redefine the KRL brand
2. Develop Internal marketing
3. Increase visibility and awareness of the KRL brand
4. Strengthen relationships between PR and KRL Staff

1. Redefine the KRL Brand	
Strategy 1: Define a **mission, vision** and **value system** that is powerful, simplified and can be internalized by staff and supporters.	
Activity 1:	Develop shared values out of what we would like to be and the collective input of staff's personal values.
Activity 2:	Identify the perceptions of internal and external stakeholders.
Activity 3:	Conduct interviews with key organizational leaders to understand their perception of the organization.
Activity 4:	Use research and shared values to develop a memorable, concise mission statement that will help guide decisions about priorities, actions and responsibilities.
Activity 5:	Use mission, shared values and research to develop a vision for KRL.
Strategy 2: Create a new **brand identity strategy** that reflects and reintroduces the essence, history, and mission of KRL.	

Figure 1.1.   Goals, strategies, and activities.

has access to or who has been collecting data in the past. It may be that certain types of data have not been consistently collected. The marketing plan can establish standards for the collection of data. A good example of this from Kitsap Regional Library's experience was the data that was collected for its community reads program: One Book, One Community. Data had been collected to measure the growth of this program; however, there was no system in place to compare data collected from year to year. Because of this, there was no good way to measure the effectiveness of changes to the program or marketing for the program. In the marketing plan, the types of data that were needed were identified *along with* the parameters for how the data would be collected.

There are a number of data points that can be tracked fairly easily without additional cost and tools. Changes in any of these numbers can indicate success or a need for further work. These may include:

• Program attendance statistics
• Circulation statistics
• Social media statistics
• Number of active cardholders: usage in the last year, usage in the last three years
• Number of new cardholders
• Number of newly inactive cardholders
• Percentage increase in use of social media

- Door counts
- Web visits
- Donations
- Number of volunteers
- Statistics on specific programs
- Statistics on specific marketing initiatives
- Number of holds on a particular item
- Number of hits on a Web page
- Google Analytics
- Surveys

All of the above involve use of simple numerical counts, except surveys. It is helpful to set up a survey schedule. Create a number of surveys that are crafted to answer questions in your priority areas. It may be necessary to adjust or add questions from year to year, but aim for consistency. Survey patrons for an awareness of products and services that are offered, as well as their level of satisfaction with their experience. Survey staff for their level of job satisfaction, knowledge of products and services, and an understanding of the goals behind key programs, initiative, and organizational goals. Surveys can also be used to reach non-users to gain a better understanding of how the community as a whole perceives the library, though gaining access to non-users tends to be more resource intensive. Focus on surveys and data that relate most closely to the goals outlined in Section 4. Be consistent in collecting the same data multiple times to measure whether the activities in each strategy are achieving the intended results.

Section 6: Budget

This section is pretty cut-and-dry. Outline the funds available. Explore funds assigned to marketing, including any funds that might be obtained through outside sources such as a foundation or friends groups. Be sure to include any award or grant funding as well.

Outline your activities from Section 4, along with the timeline in which you plan to accomplish each, and estimate how much of the budget will be needed to achieve each goal.

An added bonus of a well-crafted marketing plan is the ability to use it as a tool to build a case for funding to support the marketing efforts. The marketing plan not only helps to clarify the organization's priorities, it also becomes a clear road map for how those priorities can be supported and accomplished with strong marketing. In the process of building Kitsap Regional Library's marketing plan, the costs and benefits of rebranding the organization were outlined and have led to reprioritizing the funding to make it happen.

CONCLUSION: WORK THE PLAN

If you can answer all of the questions at the beginning of this chapter, or your marketing plan has outlined a way to get the answers, then your research and planning are done and you are ready to start working the plan. Remember that a marketing plan is a guide, but it is also the foundation for great marketing. Part of great marketing is reviewing the results of your marketing and knowing when to make a course correction. Make sure that part of your plan includes a periodic review and update of the original plan.

It is tempting to focus all of your energy into the marketing that is already in place, but that is reactionary. It is easy to want to dive right into what seems like a clever campaign, gaining the library a headline or two and its fifteen minutes of fame. Developing a marketing plan is a lot of work. Some may consider it more of a luxury than a necessity. A strong argument could be made that until you have gone through the process of developing a plan, you cannot truly understand why you are marketing. Without a marketing plan, you are simply promoting a thing: this product, that program, a new service. With a marketing plan, you have focused goals, and all of the things you do work well together, singing in concert, to build an awareness of the library in a way that no single approach can.

Chapter Two

Conversations

Building Relationships and Using Constituent Voice in Outreach

Letha Kay Goger—University of California, Merced Library

BACKGROUND: OUR FIRST TEN YEARS

The University of California (UC), Merced Library is a young library. Opening its doors to students in August of 2005, the library is the center of life at the first new research university of the twenty-first century. The library environment is open and appealing and a hub for technology on campus, designed to support a range of activities from individual research, to collaboration with peers and students, to creating and storing information. The library building is well designed, technologically rich, and well suited to support an actively growing university.

Within this young environment, library leadership has built services, collections, and tools that equal those available at its older UC sister campuses. Birthed at the same time that availability to collections of digital resources skyrocketed and became the new norm, the library provides access to almost four million e-books and one hundred thousand online journals. Although the young UC Merced Library has a relatively small print collection, researchers in the campus community also have access to one of the largest shared print collections in the world through interlibrary loan across the University of California system.

From its beginnings, the library has been unencumbered by long-held traditions and practices resistant to change that may be present in other academic libraries. It does not have rooms of aging print collections, inflexible building spaces, or outdated institutional governance structures that hinder and slow development. As such, in its first ten years, and at a time when the information landscape was changing rapidly and academic libraries were encouraged to "think like a start-up" and to implement breakthrough, paradigm-shifting, transformative, and disruptive ideas, the UC Merced Library had the freedom to do so.

During its start-up period, California and the UC Merced Library faced unprecedented budget cuts, and in a young and growing research university, there were very strong competing demands for what financial resources were available on campus. Alongside this, as with all academic libraries, new or old, the library faced competition from alternative information sources and the changing way that information is accessed and distributed. UC Merced Library, as with all libraries, exists in a very competitive reality, both on campus and within the larger information universe.

Touted as "Not what other research libraries are, what they will be," the UC Merced Library has emerged as a leader in innovation and efficiency, both by necessity and aspiration. Although it is young and there is still much development work to be undertaken, focus group studies and surveys show that both faculty and students on campus appreciate the library. Within this growing environment with its many competing interests and limited financial resources, we have learned that our best advocates for building understanding of the value of the library and for advancing library programs are the voices of our own faculty, speaking to their peers and advocating for the library resources and the information services that they need.

OPEN ACCESS POLICY: NEW INITIATIVE AND OUTREACH

In July 2013, the Academic Senate of the University of California adopted an open access (OA) policy (http://osc.universityofcalifornia.edu/open-access-policy/) in order to ensure that scholarly articles authored by faculty at its ten campuses would be made available to the public at no charge. In order to support smooth implementation of the policy, the California Digital Library (CDL), a partnership between the Office of the President of the University of California and its ten campus libraries, implemented a set of tools and resources to support the UC Open Access Policy and help its campuses and faculty to deposit their scholarly articles in eScholarship (https://escholar ship.org), UC's open access repository.

Publishing academic research with open access rights is valuable and has many benefits that can accelerate innovation and research. At the same time, publishing research with open access rights challenges traditional publishing models, including blurring traditional avenues for the advancement of ladder-rank faculty, along with posing many questions that must be answered about how authors retain and assign rights for the use of their work. The pathway to open access requires considerable education and outreach in order to engage faculty and shift academic publishing traditions and practice.

Libraries across the UC system were charged with engaging the faculty in the open access publishing movement. In order to encourage UC Merced scholars to embrace the model, the UC Merced Library initiated an outreach campaign to educate and engage faculty. Because of the vigorous debate about open access in scholarly communication, UC Merced librarians decided that faculty voices would be stronger than librarian voices for reaching their peers and speaking as advocates for this emergent practice and related library services.

Merced librarians saw the UC Open Access Policy as a perfect opportunity for engaging faculty to be a strong outreach voice in advancing open access publishing and the library services available to support faculty engagement. In order to engage faculty in such a way, library staff created a *conversation* with them.

Outreach Conversations: Engage, Don't Push

The UC Merced Library Strategic Plan calls for increased faculty and library engagement with open access publishing, and the library Communication Plan builds a pathway for two-way engagement for the library and its constituents. Through two-way communication and engagement, the UC Merced Library is able to express its value to users, to hear their research needs and aspirations, and to respond appropriately. Two-way communication and engagement also ensures that outreach and promotion efforts are targeted and authentic, focused more on engaging with the community than on pushing information about the library at them.

In this case, the library's outreach and publicity aims were to build awareness of the University of California's Open Access Policy and its requirements for faculty to publish in eScholarship or another open access repository, and to help faculty understand how to connect to eScholarship and library support through the UC Merced Library. The librarians also wanted to present information that would help quell faculty reticence toward publishing their research with open access rights, and hoped to paint a compelling picture of the emergent open access landscape, while centering UC Merced librarians as experts to support faculty in a successful transition toward open access publishing.

Because of the scope of the policy and its impact on faculty practice, librarians realized that faculty input and support were critical to these outreach efforts. The main objective here was to find and develop an authentic faculty voice that could speak to their peers about issues surrounding open access publishing, using video as the format for capturing faculty voices because the videos could be shared broadly across campus via the library's communication channels, as well as shared with others across the University of California system.

Seed Your Outreach: Communication Implies Relationship

Fortunately, and unbeknownst to us, during the previous year, we had seeded our envisioned outreach when the library provided financial support to UC Merced faculty and graduate students who wished to publish their scholarship openly. Because libraries are in the business of promoting increased access to knowledge, and in order to raise faculty awareness of the growing open access publishing movement, the UC Merced Library had funded scholarships to faculty and graduate students who published their scholarship with open access rights over the fall of 2013 and spring of 2014. Although the scholarships were not given in order to secure partners for future library outreach and publicity campaigns, a natural outcome of supporting faculty in their work resulted in authentic voices for our subsequent outreach efforts around the UC Open Access Policy the following year.

In the summer of 2014, librarians asked the 2013–2014 UC Merced open access scholarship recipients if they would be willing to be interviewed and filmed in order to support the library's outreach around the new UC Open Access Policy. The recipients were informed that the goal in videotaping them and using them as a voice on the issue was to increase awareness and engagement with the library and open access publishing across campus. Seven of the scholarship recipients agreed to be interviewed and filmed for the project. The librarians quickly realized the interconnected nature of relationship building and meeting user needs, to the availability of authentic faculty voices, willing to speak out on behalf of the library, its programs, and its initiatives.

Production: Creating the Open Access Campaign

UC Merced librarians were enthused and excited by the faculty response to this request and quickly moved into developing the "Conversations: Open Access" campaign. The instruction and scholarly communications librarian led campaign development efforts and was able to successfully recruit a large number of the faculty she had previously worked with in their open access publishing efforts. She also successfully engaged the support of the campus video producer through the University Communications office.

Coordinating interview filming times with faculty proved to be one of the more challenging aspects of the entire project. We scheduled a thirty-minute interview session with each faculty member and tried to back interviews up to each other in order to optimize the video production team's time. Arrangements were made with library administrators in order to free up certain areas in the busy library to film the conversations.

Interview questions were built beforehand and were structured to elicit narrative responses from the interviewees and to not allow for simple yes or no answers. As an example, instead of asking interviewees if they would publish again in an open access publication, which could result in a simple yes or no, the questions were constructed to expose researchers' reasons for publishing with open access, or to discover what they saw as the value of open access publications to research, innovation, and society. Examples of questions that would elicit a narrative response are, "What is the value to you of publishing via open access?" and "As faculty increasingly publish their work with open access terms of use, what will be the benefit to society or other researchers?"

Each interviewee was asked the same set of questions and, to our delight, there was a broad variety of engaging responses from the faculty. Initially, the intent was to create only one two-minute video that synthesized all of the faculty responses into a compelling single argument for open access publishing through eScholarship with library support, but since so much more positive feedback was captured on tape than expected, librarians decided to publish seven individual videos, each including the strongest sound bite from the seven faculty members. As an introduction to the campaign, our video producer also created a motion graphic video, *Generation Open* (http://youtu.be/8hxKH3-42U0), aimed to inspire the imagination as well as build interest in the seven faculty videos in the series.

Extending Reach: Campaign Dissemination and Community Engagement

The videos produced for the "Conversations: Open Access" campaign are housed on both the UC Merced and UC Merced Library YouTube accounts. This resulted in the analytics on video views being split between the channels. In the future, we will house video campaigns on only one campus channel and create a linked playlist from that channel on the other. This will ensure accurate analytics on the video views and not confuse data gathered on the campaign.

During Open Access Week 2014, the library began posting and linking to the videos through its social media channels, Facebook and Twitter. Additionally, in order to provide leadership across the University of California system, and to build knowledge and practice around open access publishing more broadly, the library offered the motion graphic video *Generation Open* for other universities and institutions to link to, download, and use in their campaigns. Within three months of posting to the International Open Access Week website (http://www.openaccessweek.org/video), this video had almost 1,200 views from around the world. The video is now the most viewed video on the Open Access Week site, a site co-sponsored by SPARC and the World Bank. We are unable to track the total number of times this video has been downloaded and reused at individual sites, but—considering that the number of views on the Open Access Week site averages between thirty and one hundred per title—this has been a tremendous success.

In addition to being distributed to other university and open publishing advocate institutions, the videos were scheduled to play on digital signage units visible to the entire UC Merced campus community. Located next to elevator landings and other high-traffic places throughout the library and student services building, these digital players place the campaign's message across our users' paths, even if they do not visit the library or are not connected via social media. Furthermore, the video campaign not only educates faculty and graduate students about publishing in an open access manor, but it builds awareness and knowledge in UC Merced's undergraduate students. The librarians anticipate that undergraduate exposure to open access publishing models early in their academic career will develop a cadre of open access advocates and emerging scholars who will be ready to fully embrace the call to open access publishing in the very near future.

Locally, librarians discovered that not only did faculty become advocates in the production of video campaigns, but faculty also reposted and shared the videos once they were published, extending the library's outreach into faculty social networks. Across the University of California system, several UC libraries also included the introductory video in their Open Access Week 2014 campaigns. Globally, the introductory video produced for the series was widely viewed, and analytics show that the views on the faculty videos are coming not only from California, but also from across the United States and the world. As such, our impact is much broader than simply educating our local university community. Social media and openly licensing our video has extended the library's reach in ways not yet evaluated.

EXPANDING THE CONVERSATION

UC Merced librarians have a sense of adventure about engaging in an authentic conversation with our constituents because we believe it will result in increased relevancy of our work and further engagement by our community with the library. We are very interested in the concept of outreach through relationships. Numerous authors discuss the importance of ensuring that libraries are satisfying a need and not just simply promoting what they are already doing. The librarians strongly believe that this relationship/conversation approach to outreach will uncover clients' needs and also demonstrate the ways they can support the library in its efforts, and vice versa.

The UC Merced Library currently has two more "Conversations" campaigns in production. One campaign is aimed to build awareness on campus of the future of academic libraries, and the other is designed to poise the library as the center of conversation on campus around information, research, and society. In the first instance, "Conversations: Academic Library Challenges, Opportunities, Futures," we are introducing library voices into the conversation, beginning with that of the interim university librarian. In this three-video series, he addresses the challenges, opportunities, and future of academic libraries. This will be followed by a four-video series, "Conversations: Information, Research and Society," in which faculty members from across the disciplines are highlighted as they discuss their research and share the ways they use and create information during the course of their work. In the conversations, new ways of engaging with information are discussed, ranging from open access publishing, to data curation and management, to accessing digital collections, and what this means for faculty, for other researchers, and for society.

Faculty are quite receptive to participating in these videos because the focus of our conversation with them is on relevant discussion points and because the videos are of high production value and reflect well on their work. The UC Merced Library is already in the preplanning stage for the second set of faculty interviews for next year's "Conversations: Information, Research and Society" video series.

In addition to working with faculty, librarians are developing student voices to speak about library services, and have produced an initial video that speaks to undergraduate students about the library's peer-supported Roving Reference service. This video was produced entirely by library student assistants and includes interviews with the Library Rovers, students who are specially trained to provide reference assistance and direction to their peers.

ASSESSING OUR EFFORTS

It is logical that faculty and students will better use a library that is understood and visible. The library's "Conversations" efforts are relatively new, and so extensive feedback and data from which to begin to understand their impact does not yet exist; however, efforts are under way for building measures into our campaigns that will help assess their effectiveness and impact.

In all of our outreach efforts, librarians use a variety of measures and feedback mechanisms to understand to what degree users find our efforts useful for building awareness and engagement with library resources, services, events, and information that they need and that are relevant to their research. The four primary mechanisms used are the following: action object mapping; focus group feedback; survey responses; and data gathering from media views, downloads, and site visitors. All of these mechanisms will help library staff understand the effectiveness of the "Conversations" campaigns.

UC Merced librarians look at each media component produced as an object that falls into a certain outreach category. Examples of categories are academic publishing, library event, and research skills workshop, and they are all aligned to overall library goals. Each outreach effort or social media post or video is mapped to these categories, and user interactions with the object are then further evaluated for effectiveness with the intended audience by user type and type of interaction. If a video is posted in social media, these interactions are likes, retweets, stars, comments, shares, and so on. In the case of our "Conversations" campaigns, librarians also use these measures to see if there are interactions with the outreach object in social media channels, including on the library's YouTube account.

Librarians also rely heavily on focus group feedback to understand how outreach efforts (i.e., video campaigns, social media posts, and other promotion efforts) build awareness and engagement with the library. During yearly focus group sessions, users are asked how they first became aware of specific new library services, resources, and workshops. They are also asked to share their favorite communication channel for receiving information about the library and why they prefer that channel.

LESSONS LEARNED

Each institution will want to discover the unique avenues and opportunities it can explore and exploit in order to better engage with its constituency as advocates for their library. One of our guiding principles is to use the audiences' unique and authentic voice to speak on the library's behalf. As such, UC Merced librarians offer the following items as principles for engaging in a campaign similar to our "Conversations" campaigns, rather than a hard-and-fast map for developing your campaign.

Ensure Authenticity of the Message

Only engage where there has been authentic work to speak about. Be real and let your constituents be. People don't want to be part of an "advertisement." Faculty who agree to engage in library promotions and campaigns are, in a very real sense, putting their professional reputations on the line to be a voice on your behalf. Be prepared to hear faculty say things you don't especially want them to say and consider freedom of expression to be part of the bargain. The success of your reputation, and theirs, depends on authentic engagement and providing them with the opportunity to speak with authority about areas that are highly relevant to their peers. Faculty will not engage if the topic you ask them to speak to is not relevant to their discipline, profession, or peers.

Cultivate Partnership Opportunities for Outreach and Publicity

See every relationship and step of work as a seed that may grow into an opportunity to develop a constituent voice that will speak on behalf of the library. Initially begun with a set of videos using faculty who previously published with open access funds and tools provided by the library, the collaboration and outreach was then extended to a video conversation with the interim university librarian, and this ultimately resulted in the process of publishing video conversations with faculty about use of library resources in their work. The initial faculty in these interviews were friends and frequent users of the library and individuals with whom we have worked in some capacity, either providing classroom instruction, scholarly publication support, data curation, collection development, or in any one of many other ways.

Outline Production Goals, but Don't Script

Faculty members who were interviewed for our "Conversations" series very much appreciated knowing the goals of the project beforehand, as well as the nature of the interview questions. Obviously, faculty do not want to be blindsided on film! As such, librarians gave them a fairly comprehensive outline of the goals of the campaign and how their work is related. At the same time, exact questions were not provided because the librarians wanted faculty responses to be spontaneous, unscripted, and organic. Each faculty member is briefed prior to the filming session and told that they can stop at any point in the interview and decline to answer a question; furthermore, they are told that they will be given an opportunity to add any additional information they may want to share, correct, or expand upon at the end of the interview session.

Make It Easy to Engage

All individuals on the UC Merced campus are extremely busy. Faculty, although willing participants, have very full calendars, heavy travel requirements, and very limited time to engage with library personnel. Coordinating video production with the faculty, the library staff, and the video production team was time intensive. This became more of an issue when, following the taping, additional filming was required in order to provide "B-roll" (additional shots that are inserted between sound bites) to enhance the video with images of the faculty member in the field, teaching, working in a lab, and so on. When the project initially began, library staff were unaware of the additional work required to shoot "B-roll." In subsequent projects, the shooting of B-roll will occur at the same time as the interview, as much as possible.

Ensure Reciprocity

Key to the "Conversations" campaigns is the idea that we want to really dig into and understand the work of the researchers on campus and how they use and create information. This is central to every message. The goal is to build awareness of the importance of their research and to extend their presence on campus at the same time they are advancing the library's work and initiatives. Librarians are working to build relationships that help both the researcher and the library be more visible and engaged, while at the same time demonstrating the relevance of the library's work to other researchers more broadly. Faculty will enthusiastically engage when our work highlights their research and supports their professional goals.

Guarantee High Production Value

Twenty-first-century audiences expect quality production, and participants expect to be portrayed attractively through text, images, and audio. As much as possible, it's important to engage with professionals who can provide professional results. UC Merced has the benefit of a professional video producer available through the campus communications department. The university video producer saved the librarians untold hours of unnecessary work and upped the production value of our films by helping everyone understand best practices for filming and for structuring interviews. His suggestions ranged from how to construct the interview questions, to how to poise ourselves as interviewers, to how to choose the best location for the filming— even down to asking the interviewees not to wear checks or small stripes when in front of the camera in order to reduce visual distortion! If an institution does not have in-house professional video production expertise, perhaps this is an opportunity to seek a donation of professional time or to build administration awareness of the need for professional support in the form of videography, photography, graphic design services, or needed equipment, if the desired outcome is professional outreach media.

Allow Adequate Time for Production

It is easy to severely underestimate the amount of time required for producing a video series, and the UC Merced Library's "Conversations" video series was no exception to that rule. Video production requires a significant investment of staff time. Some of the "Conversations" videos were produced to support initiatives with concrete deadlines. This put the librarians under severe pressure, and the quality of the videos produced under pressure suffered! Moving forward, librarians have become more efficient in the planning process, resulting in fewer production surprises. Library administration is committed to supporting future campaigns and sees them as effective. At the same time, our library staff are spread very thin, and the number of videos in each campaign series must be limited due to the impact video production has on staff time.

Disseminate Broadly and Across Open Channels

Ensure there is a plan for postproduction dissemination and optimize the opportunity to use the media that is produced across all library channels, both formal and social media. Videos were embedded in library e-mail newsletters and social media, linked to the library website home page, included on the university open access information site, and distributed to colleagues to use and reuse at other universities in their 2014 Open Access Week campaigns. The International Monetary Fund, a major sponsor for open access across the developing world, used one of the UC Merced Library's videos to open its 2014 Open Access Week campaign on its Twitter channel—this speaks to the value of distributing high-value content broadly and openly and of the potential reach of locally produced content.

Continue the Connection

UC Merced faculty really appreciated follow-up correspondence on the status of production, timelines, and next steps. In one case, due to an unexpected family illness with a primary library team member, production slowed down considerably for a period of several months. During this time, we did not just drop from the scene but, rather, communicated with faculty, who more than understood about the production delay. General courtesy went a long way in this process and eased our path when production lagged or there was a need for additional video shoots and engagement with faculty members.

Build New Engagements

The UC Merced Library staff are building a culture of using our constituents' voices in our outreach work. One goal is to provide new channels of connecting through our work relationships and then building upon that in our outreach efforts. We expect that as faculty see themselves as central to the library work and message, they will increasingly imagine and anticipate how they can more fully support our work, as we support theirs. Another goal is to always be creating new pathways to engagement through our relationship building. This will meet our library objectives and, at the same time, create a perpetual flow of new material to use in outreach and promotion work.

CONCLUSION

As competition for faculty attention increases across the information universe, it is important to increasingly reorient the library's eye toward seeing clients as the starting point, rather than as the end service point. Likewise, we must center the library as the research hub on campus, as well as *the* place where conversations about information, research, and society occur, as these conversations will help the library comprehend and appreciate the research occurring on campus and provide the forum for expressing the library's role in making it happen.

Throughout the literature, the concept of communication lines up well with the concept of value—through conversation, relationships are developed and become valued; valued services are those that are needed and that develop or are realized through relationships. In the case of the "Conversations: Open Access Policy" campaign, the UC Merced scholarly communications librarian established a relationship by providing support to university faculty who were interested in publishing their scholarly works with open access licenses. In return, those faculty were willing to be advocates for the library in a campaign developed to build awareness and engagement across the campus with open access publishing and the university's open access repository.

There is no way to separate library outreach from customer relationships. Gone are the days when a library can push their messages toward users and expect them to engage just because the library is the only game in town. It is only when we develop and promote resources, services, and tools that are truly needed that we can legitimately and organically champion the library and what it does. Building relationships and using our constituents' voices to speak to their peers is one of the strongest models when speaking to faculty in an academic research university.

No one can accomplish great things alone, and this is nowhere more true than in the university community. At UC Merced Library, we are using conversations to help change our orientation from pushing products at our community, to engaging with users in organic ways. We are trusting that if relationships are done right, publicity and outreach will emerge in ways that spark true interest and that introduce new life and ideas about the library and its role across the campus. Through these campaigns, librarians are endeavoring to strengthen relationships with clients and to further build the library's future as the center of conversation on campus around information, research, and society.

ACKNOWLEDGMENTS

Thank you to Donald Barclay, interim university librarian, for his leadership and encouragement to engage in authentic conversation. I recognize Susan Mikkelsen, UC Merced instruction and scholarly communications librarian, for the foundational work she has done to build a culture of open access publishing and conversation around scholarly communication on the University of California, Merced, campus. Similarly, I recognize the professional expertise and production support received from Jürgen Gottschalk, video producer in the Communications Department at UC Merced. Ongoing work to build high-quality outreach campaigns on video would not be possible or successful without the support and encouragement received from the UC Merced Communications team.

Chapter Three

Plano Public Library System

Building a Social Media Presence

Brent Bloechle — Plano Public Library System

INTRODUCTION

The Plano Public Library System (PPLS) in Plano, Texas, comprises five libraries of approximately 30,000 square feet each and serves a population of 270,000 people. PPLS has a very active and engaged social media program. By the end of 2014, almost 40 percent (68) of the 174 staff members were contributing to the libraries' social media presence by posting library-related information and other content, creating educational videos, or writing reviews. The most vital part of PPLS's social media program is the committed staff members with their creativity and willingness to try out new ideas, as well as share and teach one another, because without them, nothing would be possible.

If you are just getting started with social media, or already at the point of expanding your social media presence, the most crucial part of any campaign is the people that represent your library. The thirteen separate social media platforms PPLS supports are each directed by a professional librarian. They oversee support groups or committees that range in size from five to fifteen staff members. These groups are composed of a mix of both professional librarians and nonprofessional staff members. Each of these groups is solely responsible for the content on their respective platform. Much of the uptake of new social media is driven by staff members who identify sites that are popular with the public; they then organize a group of other staff members who are interested in supporting participation on that new platform. The committee then brings the idea to the library system management. Before any social media project is initiated, a business plan is developed that identifies the following criteria: the number of staff members needed to support a high-quality presence, the target audience to be engaged, the frequency of posts, the types of posts, and the goal for usage by the public. All the committees are charged with three objectives: to promote the library system's activities and services, to educate the community, and to connect with and engage the public.

Public engagement by the Plano Public Library System began in January 2008 with one blog called *PlanoReads* on the WordPress platform. This was followed in spring 2009 with the *infoLinks* blog, also on WordPress. These initial forays into social media gave the library system's management the information necessary to gauge patron response to professionally developed content and to determine whether it was possible to create additional opportunities for community engagement via social media. In February 2010, PPLS ventured onto its first social media platform where patrons could connect with us in two-way conversations by joining us on Facebook.

Because of the success of these three early efforts, over the next five years, PPLS added four additional blogs and six additional social media sites that staff members now actively support. The blogs, the social media sites, and the Plano Public Library website (http://www.planolibrary.org) are all interlinked in supporting engagement with the citizens of Plano and the surrounding communities, as well as thirty-two countries, per statistics obtained through Facebook. According to the latest Pew Research Internet Project statistics (Duggan et al., 2015), the younger, more ethnically diverse audience wants their social media available on mobile platforms; PPLS anticipated this at the end of 2013 with the launch of the library system's mobile app in order to better support those who are connecting via tablets and smartphones. This fit perfectly with PPLS's goals, since the city of Plano is a very diverse community with over eighty-eight languages spoken in the Plano Public School District. Another goal of all of the content that PPLS creates is to use that content on multiple social media platforms, and to ensure that content is accessible for easy retrieval for future posts and other projects. Our expectation for created materials is to have a longer shelf life than the immediacy of an initial posting.

PPLS BLOGS

Initially, the *PlanoReads* blog was only used as a location for PPLS librarians to post their book recommendations and staff-written reviews of materials within the library system's collection. At first, library staff were hesitant to accept reviews from the public; concerns were with the quality of the writing and the potential for controversial reviews. The blog now accepts reviews from the public, and no problems have been experienced. From the outset, the blog provided a forum for information about the four PPLS book clubs, though its uses have grown and evolved since its original inception. The staff members now include reviews on all material types in the PPLS collection, including movies, audio books, and music, as well as video book reviews. As staff have gained confidence and the necessary technological skills, new formats are added. And as the opportunities present themselves, the blog now includes video interviews with authors conducted by PPLS staff. All video creations are posted to the PPLS YouTube channel under its own playlist, pinned on a themed Pinterest board, and promoted via Twitter.

The *infoLinks* blog was started when pathfinders or portals to information were still popular and used by the public. Undeniably, PPLS came late to this use of the Internet. The links are selected and maintained by professional librarians and include such topics as travel, health, local interest, and employment. Over time, as we've learned that the public is happy with "good enough" Google-like results, admittedly use of the links has declined. The peak usage year for *infoLinks* was 2011 with 20,889 views. However, PPLS still supports *infoLinks* because the information housed on the blog is then repurposed for use on other social media outlets. This blog is also the location for more topical information. In 2014, the most popular areas were for information on tax preparation and on the elections. Information on the Affordable Care Act and Ebola were two topical subjects that the staff created and then vetted with relevant information links. These pages were then linked to other PPLS social media outlets. As the library system moves forward with these social media activities, the role this blog will play will be reevaluated. During the height of the recession and because of the demand, employment information was divided into a separate blog called *PPLS Job Center*.

The *Kids' Brain* blog has the largest and most consistent viewership— though, as with the other blogs, it has declined somewhat in usage, it still maintains a strong audience, just not as big as it once was at over 35,000 views in 2012. The blog is successful by including a wide range of child-focused information, including reviews on books, music, movies, and computer apps. The staff have developed a collection of video and audio literacy tips that are linked to the blog from the PPLS YouTube channel. The staff also produce a collection of library puppet shows that support literacy and entertain our youngest patrons. These posts demonstrate and share information from PPLS live programming. It is important to provide this direct connection to patrons. This supports the objective of Plano's virtual "Sixth Library" by bringing the library experience to patrons wherever they may be. This blog supports many cross-posts with book reviews, literacy videos, podcasts, and video book reviews, and it is linked to Facebook, Pinterest, Twitter, and YouTube. Facebook features a weekly literacy tip from the *Kids' Brain* blog each Monday. The favorite apps have a board on Pinterest.

One of the more popular posts is the book reviews done by the kids them-selves. Each library has book review slips, and the children write out their reviews, consisting of one or two sentences, and drop them in the box on the children's reference desk. A staff member reviews and posts the items on the blog. They are presented in blocks of three to six with the image of the book cover next to the review to stimulate interest.

Plano Teens Connect! is a blog that provides young adult book, movie, and music reviews, as well as reviews by teens. There are links to homework help and games. The focus for the most part is on lists of suggested titles by genre and includes information about the teen book club, Plano Bibliovores. The staff also post images and videos of teen programming. The professional staff have ascertained that the level of usage on this blog has decreased somewhat, and they are in the process of shifting posting priorities to Tumblr instead. However, the blog will continue to host book reviews and other material that can be linked to or reposted onto Tumblr. A decision was made to retain the information on the blog because of the fast turnover of Tumblr posts, and its existence on the blog ensures easier retrieval for future use.

The *Genealogy* blog supports the community outreach of the PPLS Gene-alogy Center and promotes new materials and programs. The *Genealogy* blog and website are the portals to unique historical collections owned by the Plano Public Library System. Using CONTENTdm, the staff of the Genealo-gy Center provide public access to explore the history of the city of Plano and surrounding Collin County. Links are provided to exclusive digitized collections of photographs, documents, family histories, and other historical information, dating back to the late 1800s. The blog regularly features selec-tions from these collections to generate public interest and direct patrons to access points on the PPLS website (see figure 3.1).

The *PPLS Job Center* provides information and links to assistive services for job searching, interview preparation, and résumé writing. The *infoLinks* blog initially hosted job search information, but in 2012 it was established as a standalone blog due to high demand. The service was enhanced with regu-lar links posted to articles and information on how to search for jobs and get hired for a job. Lists of job fairs and networking opportunities are regularly included, as are links to such PPLS-provided databases as LearningExpress and Reference USA. PPLS provides live computer skills training classes, in-person job searching seminars, and the use of PPLS-assisted Skype inter-views, and these are all listed on the blog.

Over the last few years, these blogs have seen less use, with peak use occurring in 2012 at 118,647 views. Even with less usage, over the past two years the blogs regularly average from 3,500 to 4,000 views per month. Library staff members attribute some of the reduction in views to a change in what the public wants to use, along with easier access from other sources for reviews. With the surging use of the PPLS Twitter page and the quick growth

https://glhtainplano.wordpress.com

Feeds: Posts Comments

MATTHEWS – Henry C. and Mary A. — My Quest For the Truth
January 16, 2015 by plato1973

For years I have been told that my 2nd great-grandfather and mother (Henry C. Matthews and Mary Ann Davidson) are buried in the Bear Creek Cemetery in Adair County, Missouri. Henry was born in Lexington, Fayette, Kentucky to Daniel and Rachel Matthews. Mary Ann Davidson, was born in Indiana or Missouri or Tennessee. (Three different records and three different locations.)

ABOUT US
Genealogy Center is updated by the genealogy staff of the Plano Public Library System in Plano, Texas. If you have any questions or suggestions, please contact Cheryl Smith, cheryls@plano.gov

Figure 3.1. The genealogy blog featuring examples from the PPLS collection of historical photographs. Plano Public Library System staff.

experienced with Instagram, the public may be letting library staff know that quicker and faster with less depth is what they prefer. Some of the reduction can also be attributed to how the library system promotes the blogs online. The blogs had direct links from the PPLS website home page for several years. Since the library's website is part of the online presence of the City of Plano, when the city revamped the entire website in 2013, the library's home page needed to be altered as well. As part of the revamp, the landing page length for all departments was reduced so that they would all have a similar look and feel. This resulted in the library blogs being moved to a link on a sidebar with substantially less visibility. The reduction in visibility seems to have translated directly into fewer views. As with most things, out-of-sight results in lower awareness and, in this case, less use.

SOCIAL MEDIA: MOVING BEYOND BLOGS

Between 2008 and 2010, as the recession deepened, PPLS staff identified social media activities as a way to engage with the public, provide information, and educate library users about the library's services and collection.

With the advent of increased digital materials and information, the challenge was to find other ways to connect and stay relevant in this changing service environment. PPLS had consistently large attendance at its programs. For example, in 2009, the library system held 1,916 programs with an attendance of 77,188. But, in 2010, PPLS identified a need to find additional ways to engage with the community and build greater awareness of services and programs since just a fraction of the potential service population of 270,000 attended programs. Accordingly, the library system pursued social media as a way to connect with this underserved audience. By 2014, the number of programs had grown to 3,063 with attendance at well over 115,520. As the PPLS social media presence and use of the online catalog grew, the perception of these endeavors changed from being isolated activities separated from one another to a single entity, what staff came to call the PPLS Sixth Library. The library system needed to be where patrons were—and they were online. Thus, it was important to provide those who connect to the library online with as many of the same services as they would experience if they physically walked into a building. Failure to provide a strong, multisite approach would result in not staying relevant to users in the future.

The Plano Public Library System has very simple but specific guidelines that are common across all social media platforms. What PPLS uses:

- Posts about upcoming events
- Links to other social media outlets, such as Twitter, Facebook, etc.
- Communications with patrons, authors, other libraries, and organizations
- Relevant information, such as closings, new services, and related news
- Items that followers may find interesting and that don't fall under the "do not post" list

What PPLS does not post:

- Anything vulgar, profane, or disrespectful
- Political or religious pictures
- Personal opinions (remember, you are representing PPLS, not yourself)

Obviously, the guidelines above are somewhat nebulous. Therefore, PPLS staff believe that a good thought to keep in mind when using any social media platform—before hitting "send," "post," "enter," etc.—is to imagine the staff member's name and photo posted next to his or her online comments or pictures. Then the staff member should ask her- or himself: Does it *still* seem like a good idea? Is this being a good PPLS representative? Poorly drafted or unintentional comments can create ethical dilemmas and embarrass the library system *and* the staff member making the posts. Since social media posts are fairly permanent and can go viral within a matter of days, inappropriate postings can create immediate and lasting damage. Although committee members are tasked with following the current PPLS guidelines for social media and to ask questions as needed, if there's any doubt about the appropriateness, the recommendation is not to post.

Facebook

Besides the blogs, Facebook was the initial social site that PPLS created. The first post to the PPLS Facebook page was on February 15, 2010. Posting started with a small, hesitant group of staff that was somewhat uneasy about what they were doing. Much of the concern was over the immediacy of the posts, but with practice, their comfort level and confidence grew. Initially, a variety of posts were tried, but as PPLS's following increased and using demographics provided by Facebook, staff members were better able to identify and target posts to the audience. The broad selection of topics tried—science news, book reviews, trivia, and library happenings—were based at first on a staff member's personal interests and knowledge. By studying which posts generated likes, comments, and shares, it became easier to determine what would resonate with patrons. Early on, the interest was in book reviews, library programs, information about children's literacy, and book-related trivia and information. These were broken up with entertaining humor and current cultural happenings, avoiding at all times the possibility of any type of controversy.

During PPLS's first year on Facebook, the Facebook group began structured weekly posts to see if the public could be enticed back with periodic and predictable postings. Tuesday Titles was initiated as the first such series of postings done weekly. With Tuesday Titles, the public provides an author and the staff suggest three similar authors. Staff were initially concerned that they would become overwhelmed with requests, but this proved not to be the case. This program continues, and on most Tuesdays, there are one to four requests, which can easily be answered within an appropriate time frame. The *PlanoReads* blog team and the Facebook group work together to support the Tuesday Titles effort. During that first year, the statistics from Facebook analytics indicated that 80 percent of PPLS followers were women in the eighteen-to-fifty-four age range. With this information, the Facebook team began to tailor the postings to appeal more to this demographic. Posts of wider interest are still included less frequently, but the staff made a conscious decision to enable closer engagement with our core audience.

At the outset of this foray into social media, the Plano Public Library System did not have a staff support team in place to create library-developed posts. Over the past five years, the staff engagement in social media has grown, as has the library of staff-created materials that can be drawn from to create original posts. The staff also draw upon a wide variety of sources to connect patrons with information of interest beyond what the library can directly create. It is important to include materials that are developed in-house, especially video productions, so the public can have a visual connection with a librarian that they may see during a visit or presenting a program they may attend. Over the next several years, additional regularly posted topics were developed: Monday Literacy Tips, Caturday (literary cat pictures), regular links to the PPLS blogs for book reviews, and referrals to the PPLS Pinterest page for new titles.

During "Suburban Dare," which is the PPLS summer program, a video promoting the program is created in conjunction with Plano Television and is used across all of the PPLS social media sites, as well as on the City of Plano site. The production includes library staff, members of other city departments, and, for the past few years, the mayor. Facebook is the repository for the summer photo contest, which has pictures of a patron's library card on vacation in exotic locales (whether it be Grandma's house or Fiji). Photo submissions by the participants are uploaded to Facebook and then pinned to a board on Pinterest. The public can then vote for the winners. Posts to Facebook are done three to four times per day each morning, lunchtime, and evening, which are the times that patrons are most likely to check their stream (see figure 3.2). All posts are prescheduled so that they appear seven days a week, even on holidays.

Our Facebook followers often respond and post to the page on holidays when the library is closed. Facebook posts need to be of immediate interest, so information about programs is generally not posted earlier than a day before an event is scheduled. Photos taken at PPLS library programs, such as Novel Knitters and robotics, are included to help encourage the patrons to participate in future activities and engage with us.

Twitter

Twitter has by far the largest audience of the PPLS social media sites. It is also the most ephemeral. Posts are done two to five times per day with an effort made to spread them throughout the day and post at times when the public are most likely to be catching up on tweets. The posts place an emphasis on upcoming PPLS activities, book reviews, and city activities. PPLS's tweets include repostings from other PPLS social media; connecting to the various boards on Pinterest, such as the Book of the Day; literacy tips from the *Kids' Brain* blog; fun items from the PPLS Facebook page; and links to video clips on the PPLS YouTube channel. The Twitter page endeavors to redirect the public to other PPLS sites and activities that can provide more information and, hopefully, generate a longer-term connection with the patron. Our Twitter group uses Twuffer to preschedule tweets.

Figure 3.2. Fun on Facebook with a Yoda holiday tree. Plano Public Library System staff.

Pinterest

Pinterest helped to solve persistent requests from the patrons of the library system. The public asked regularly for lists of new titles for adults, teens, and children. The professional staff created boards on Pinterest for new adult fiction and nonfiction, young adult books, picture books, junior fiction and nonfiction, DVDs, and audio books. These boards are refreshed with five to ten new titles per week. While this is not all of the new materials the library system receives each week, it does serve the purpose intended. These eight new title boards form the core of the service provided on Pinterest. These boards are linked in the sidebar within the Polaris catalog under the title Best New Books & More. Each board has a box in the first row suggesting other boards the user might be interested in viewing. This is another effort at broadening the connection with patrons. The New Young Adult Titles board receives the most repins, likes, and comments. This was a surprise because when staff first started using Pinterest, they had expected an adult board would receive the most interaction. There are also twenty-three additional boards that share other materials from the library collection, as well as fun library activities. These additional boards provide more connection points to materials on blogs and other social media sites. Some of the historical images from the Genealogy Center collection are shared here, as are the adult video book reviews, photos taken at live programs, and library displays. Pinterest has a unique set of followers, and we try to connect them to library services and activities beyond board posts. The boards on Pinterest also serve as a place where the staff can be creative and share their interests. Much as a staff member might do a table display on cooking because that is an area of personal interest to them, the staff can create boards on Pinterest. They have created boards on topics as varied as Crazy Titles, Foreign Films, Library Crafts, and Library Cards from Around the World. A table display may only last for a couple of weeks or a month, but boards on Pinterest have a more lasting opportunity to find a wider audience.

YouTube

YouTube is fast becoming a major part of library social media activities, specifically because it enables staff to provide engagement with the public in support of the goals for the PPLS Sixth Library, bringing library activities and services to wherever patrons may be. Staff members currently upload video book reviews, puppet shows, literacy tips, crafts to support literacy, and activities from library programs (see figure 3.3). These are frequently on an array of topics. Staff members are fortunate to have access to three digital creation spaces, and those not in a location with a digital creation space are within a fifteen-minute drive of a library that does have one. This ease of access enables more staff members to participate and learn. The library system also works with the City of Plano's cable television channel for the creation of some videos. The cable channel also utilizes some of PPLS's videos in its broadcast schedule. The growing collection of materials allows

Figure 3.3. Examples of staff-created videos on YouTube. Plano Public Library System staff.

for regular postings to the library's website and other social media sites. The ability to reuse prior items is important so that there is not a need to always rely on new material. For example, a video created in September about how to download e-books and featured on the library website at that time was featured again post-holiday and received a fresh surge of usage.

Flickr

Flickr is used by the Plano Public Library System as a repository of photos from programs and other library activities. This collection of photographs is reused to promote future programs that are similar. The photos are generally arranged in albums, and over time they have become a sort of visual library for the history of the Plano Public Library System. The images are used on posts on Facebook, Twitter, and Instagram.

NEW SOCIAL MEDIA SITES

During 2014, the Plano Public Library System ventured into two new social media sites, Tumblr and Instagram. Staff approached participating in each of these sites as an opportunity to reach a younger audience, with most statistics indicating that over 50 percent of the audience using these two platforms is under thirty-five years of age.

Tumblr

As mentioned previously, PPLS is currently transitioning from the *Plano Teens Connect!* blog to Tumblr as the primary site for staff efforts to reach teens. Book reviews and other activities are posted to Tumblr and linked back to the blog. Teen and tween program information is also shared. A large part of what PPLS's Tumblr committee posts are reposts of items the staff believes will be entertaining to teens and reflect current teen culture. The goal is to have one out of five posts directly related to a PPLS service. Each post includes hashtags to help the public find the PPLS site. The tags included on each post are #planopubliclibrarysystemtx and #planotx, and the book reviews include #planoteensconnect. Tumblr also has consistent posts for specific days, with book reviews on Monday, Wednesday, and Friday. Each Friday, a dance video is posted. Tumblr is the only site where PPLS has posted a specific disclaimer about the content because Tumblr is very open: some avatars and names that people use could be considered objectionable. PPLS's disclaimer reads as follows:

> This Tumblr page does not represent official Plano Public Library System communications. Any links to external Internet sites do not constitute the Library's endorsement of the content of the sites or of their policies or products.

The committee members try not to repost items that may link to an objectionable site or that have potentially objectionable avatars. The hope is that the audience will take time to view the PPLS post among the other posts. This site is, as with all social media, provided with a steady feed of posts to keep the audience engaged.

Instagram

The PPLS Instagram presence began early in 2014. The objective, as with all of our social media sites, is for the Plano Public Library System to connect the public with the library's materials and services, and to promote upcoming programs. Creating engagement with patrons via images has proven to be more of a challenge. The big difference is that it is instantaneous. Instagram followers are much more likely to comment on or like a post than with any other social activity staff have engaged with. Everything posted thus far by PPLS staff has received some type of response, either a like or a comment. While working with images has been challenging, the response has been tremendously rewarding, and it appears that Instagram is connecting well with a new audience. Each post includes these three hashtags: #plano, #planotx, and #planolibrary, and the hashtag of the location where the photo was taken (see figure 3.4). Other hashtags included are descriptive of the image so that the post will have a wider reach. The committee is currently looking at themes that could be supported each week with photos or short videos, such as behind the scenes at your local library. The library uses Icono square.com to track usage. Instagram initially grew faster at the outset than any of our other social media sites. This observation is supported by statistics from a recent report from Pew Research, which indicates that Instagram is now used by 26 percent of online adults, surpassing Twitter at 23 percent, and it is gaining on LinkedIn and Pinterest, both at 28 percent (Duggan et al., 2015).

UNKNOWN PLACES

Being online always carries the potential for damage to an organization's reputation. The staff at PPLS are expected to do no harm. Your organization may not always have total control of your reputation because activities can occur beyond the posts that you do. There may be online sites where your organization is not engaged, but that does not mean that the community has not engaged there for you under your name. For example, PPLS's experiences with Foursquare and Yelp are part of our learning experience with social media. PPLS was not on Foursquare and did not have plans to be on it, but our patrons thought differently. They independently created six separate sites for the various PPLS locations. For the most part, their actions and posts were harmless fun with the public checking in at the locations, becoming the mayor of the library, and generally saying nice things about the libraries in the few posts that were created. However, one post directed the public to a link with X-rated adult materials. When this was discovered by a patron and brought to a staff member's attention, Foursquare was contacted to reclaim our name and have the offending post removed. PPLS is now on Foursquare, but not actively posting, in an effort to protect the library system's name.

Yelp is a very popular site for the public to review restaurants, services, and organizations such as libraries. The public had created sites and posted reviews for PPLS locations. Some of these posts were not complimentary or even accurate. PPLS needed to reply to these posts, but library staff could not because staff had not created the sites. Again, staff had to contact Yelp to

Figure 3.4.   An example of mixing promotional materials with library activity photos on Instagram. Plano Public Library System staff.

reclaim the PPLS name and the sites that had been opened in order to respond to the public posts. By owning the site, you can post publicly to comments but also privately to individuals. When posting responses, it is important to be accurate and careful so that a negative comment does not become worse if the person reacts negatively to your reply. PPLS Yelp sites are mostly accessed by the public for directions to the libraries, but one to two comments per week do come from the public, most of which have been positive and complimentary about the libraries, as well as our customer service. As an organization, you may or may not want to be everywhere on the Internet, but that doesn't mean you won't end up there. It is very important to regularly conduct searches to see where the public has placed your organization in social media.

CONCLUSION

Moving forward, PPLS continues to redefine its social media objectives. What is the library system's goals for social media—is it social marketing or is it library media relations? It is both, but it is also entertainment. Participation by the public in a two-way conversation with the library can be somewhat limited. Given the opportunity, the public likes and shares posts, especially if it is easy to do and instantaneous. The library's social media sites receive regular questions, although not an inordinate amount, but enough that each can be viewed as golden opportunities to engage the community. Library staff members also receive comments of praise from the public about PPLS services via social media. So while much of what staff are doing is about promoting library activities and services, there is an engagement component that must be nurtured. It can't just all be about the library, even if that is what most staff would prefer. When entertainment, humor, and items of current interest from other online sources are blended in, there is a better response to library information. As with much of society, the public is finding the niches that appeal to them, and the one-size-fits-all approach no longer serves well when reaching out to the public. It can't just be Facebook or Pinterest; each has a somewhat different audience. To engage the public, staff must complete regular posts at times that the public wants the content, not just when it is convenient for employees to engage. The library staff are continually looking at new social media sites and evaluating them to see if those sites might be where the public is going next, as the PPLS audience continues to fracture into smaller segments. Just like at one time MySpace was the place to be, some of the current sites may face the same fate. It is important not to tie your future success to only one way of connecting and engaging with the public.

REFERENCE

Duggan, Maeve, Nicole B. Ellison, Cliff Lampe, Amanda Lenhart, and Mary Madden. 2015. "Social Media Update 2014." Pew Research Center, January 9. http://www.pewinternet.org/2015/01/09/social-media-update-2014/.

Chapter Four

Creating Campus Buzz with Promotional Videos

Heather A. Dalal, Paris Hannon, and Robert J. Lackie — Rider University Libraries

BACKGROUND

Rider University is a small private university in central New Jersey, enrolling approximately five thousand students on two campuses (Lawrenceville and Princeton). The emerging technologies librarian is one of the ten library faculty members within the Moore Library, the main library at Rider University. As the newest librarian, she was hired to help the library move with the university's venture into online learning. After conducting needs assessments and settling into the university, she began working with student workers to employ instructional technologies to advertise library services and make library tutorials more effective and appealing to college students. This chapter includes a narrative of how Rider University Libraries created promotional videos, how these videos evolved from informative to dramatic, and how the newest series was marketed for increased visibility. This chapter also includes advice and best practices for librarians interested in creating their own promotional videos.

LITERATURE REVIEW

Many academic libraries have experimented with going beyond screencasted tutorials to create promotional videos. A brief article by Little (2011) described how academic libraries have used streaming video for library promotion, library orientation, information literacy instruction, and special collections. Videos have been popular and effective at reaching students and im-

proving opinions about the library (Wakiji and Thomas, 1997). Online instruction is a must for distance courses, but the same videos can supplement
face-to-face library instruction as well. Librarians spend a lot of time and
effort trying to teach information literacy instruction but at times can lose
students' attention. Promotional videos can help because their short, informative messages have been carefully written for maximum effectiveness. These
videos gather students' attention as learners remember and encode information better when it is visual and presented in a novel and remarkable way
(Thornton and Kaya, 2013). Appealing to students by evoking emotion and
humor while lecturing makes lessons more memorable (Babin, Berman, and
Kronmiller, 2013; Lo, 2011).

Examples of catchy and informative library promotional videos have been
produced by Arizona State University, California State University, and York
University. Arizona State University's The Library Minute series featured a
librarian introducing students to multiple topics related to the library and
information literacy (Perry, 2011). The Northridge Oviatt Library of California State University created a series informing faculty of resources available
to them via the library (Martin, 2012). The York University Libraries' series
of videos contained interviews with students offering advice to their peers on
college life and research (Majekodunmi and Murnaghan, 2012). Each university reported that their videos were enjoyable to watch and have been successful in reaching students.

Other promotional videos produced by libraries haves been more dramatic than informative. Ohio State University's series, Circulation, met success
because "students and instructors respond well to humorous short videos in
which we do not take ourselves too seriously" (Saines, 2011: 532). Tsinghua
University (China) produced a series of videos, Falling in Love with the
Library, and discovered that the style of this video series appealed to students
because the episodes are "the exact opposite of the serious and rigid stereo-
type of [the] library image" and are "humorous, light-hearted, and refresh-
ing" (Luo, Wang, and Han, 2013: 464). The Texas A&M library orientation
video, "The Research Games," was based on the popular books and movies
series The Hunger Games. The time spent on this project for the library was a
wise investment as the movies will remain relevant for years to come
(Schwartz, 2012). Finally, Brigham Young University Libraries have produced many promotional videos. "New Spice: Study like a Scholar" was a
parody of an Old Spice commercial that went viral all over the Internet,
having close to 3.5 million YouTube views as of January 2015 (Hbllproduc-
tion, 2010). With all of these great experiences, ideas, and publications,
pursuing a video series at Rider University seemed like an ambitious yet fun
and worthwhile project. While the reuse of promotional videos produced by
other libraries is also effective, a lot can be gained by creating videos with
the university's own branding and students; other students relate to their

friends on camera, and librarians can specify the content and improve the library's own image.

Before starting, Rider University librarians considered advice from the scholarly literature on the planning and use of videos in libraries. Librarians strongly recommended student-librarian collaborations for their effectiveness and also suggested spending a lot of time in developing a plan to have a clear goal in mind (Majekodunmi and Murnaghan, 2012; Perry, 2011; Saines, 2011), and to keep the videos short and the learning objectives limited so as not to overburden students with too much new information all at once (Mestre, 2012; Oud, 2009).

FIRST ATTEMPT AT PROMOTIONAL VIDEOS

Like most libraries, Rider University Libraries (RUL) has done little promotion to students outside of formal research instruction sessions. The most recent focus group findings indicated that even the students who come to the Moore Library daily were unaware of many RUL tools and services. The library began to produce short videos that were half tutorial and half commercial in the summer of 2013. During that time, a film and media studies major worked with the emerging technologies librarian and other student workers, training them on the process of creating videos. No new equipment was acquired; the tools needed were available to the library. Film and voice-over were captured using equipment already owned by the library, a Kodak Zi8 Pocket Video Camera. Editing of the videos was possible with Tech-Smith's Camtasia Studio, which the library had been using for screencasted tutorials.

The promotional videos quickly gathered a lot of enthusiasm among library personnel, and others became involved. The emerging technologies librarian's co-liaison partner to the School of Education and current department chairperson started to suggest themes and learning objectives and coordinate outreach to students and faculty. The library systems manager became responsible for creating library website banner advertisements and designed a technology-focused promotional video introducing the library scanners, microform machines, laptops, and photocopiers. Student workers all over the library volunteered to star in the videos. Collaboration and tapping into the creativity and talent of others has been a key factor in getting started, as all of this was very new to this librarian-student production team.

By the end of the summer in 2013, RUL offered three different series of videos, Lost in the Library (LITL), Know Your Librarian (KYL), and the main series, The Rider Libraries Minute (TRLM). LITL's focus has been on students teaching students about using the physical library. The other two series have been actively focused on the needs of distance students, remembering that distance students include those on campus who walk past the library, but never in it (Glennie and Mays, 2013; Nicholas and Tomeo, 2005). The KYL series was created to introduce librarians to students enrolled in distance programs. TRLM, the largest series, contained seventeen episodes on varying topics, including Boolean searching, interlibrary loan, empirical research, and accessing the library from off campus. TRLM episodes all have the same format: introduction, student host narrating a concept, screencasted tutorial, and then sign-off with the TRLM logo on the screen. Each is as close to a minute long as possible and covers one to two learning objectives.

These videos were all very well received. Librarians play them in research instruction and are pleased with the simplicity of the videos. TRLM received a statewide library publicity and marketing award. The reaction was satisfying, but the team had higher goals. While the librarians were pleased with the videos, they were not getting the play time, view counts, and attention desired. The team wanted to grab students' attention and increase their awareness of library resources. Something had to change.

In the summer of 2014, the team discussed RUL's marketing direction and brainstormed ideas for the next episodes of TRLM—and a new video series was envisioned. The new goals of this new series would be to take the promotional videos up a level, appeal to a broader range of students, and perhaps even become Internet famous.

ESTABLISHING GROUNDWORK FOR THE NEW SERIES

The goal of the new series is to go "viral," if not in the real world, then just on campus. Viral marketing is a technique to generate traffic to a product in the business world. This kind of marketing can be applied to libraries. Librarians wish *all* students would take advantage of library resources to save time, produce more scholarly work, and earn better grades. The previous series of videos were only reaching a fragment of the student population. Very few students were aware of the library's promotional video series, unless their classes had research instruction sessions and librarians elected to play episodes. Still, students felt reluctant to access these videos for fun or library help. The marketing need is real because upperclassmen often tell librarians that they wished they had been aware of all the library had to offer. The librarian-student team felt a strong obligation to increase awareness of the library's tools and services, so the team brainstormed ideas for quite some time before getting started.

To achieve the high marketing objectives, the team really wanted to do something pioneering. It was decided to explore a good dramatic concept that could persist in making an entire series of enjoyable videos. The team revisited a previously rejected idea of parodying movies or commercials. The team wanted to find the right blockbuster movie to serve as a springboard for the new promotional video series. It took several months, but finally the right idea emerged—this past summer's top movie, *Guardians of the Galaxy*.

The Guardians of the Library (GOTL) idea created so much excitement that scripts were composed before the team found the time to see the film in the movie theater; two scenes were written by just watching the trailers and parodies. After seeing the full movie, the team felt confident about the decision to begin the GOTL series and enthusiastically moved forward to create these videos. Since Marvel Studios has planned a sequel for 2017, these videos will stay relevant for years. The project received support from the dean of the university libraries, the Moore Library department chairperson, and almost everyone employed by RUL, so work began in earnest on the new series.

PROCESS OF CREATING VIDEOS

The most exhilarating aspect of producing these videos was that the team attempted to perform every Hollywood job there is: casting, directing, editing, producing, script writing, set design, filming, costumes, and makeup. The team was able to build upon the process established when creating the TRLM, LITL, and KYL series, and the students and librarians have been able to complete each part of the process collaboratively.

The Story and Script

The process for creating the informative promotional videos would often begin with a learning objective and then the student-librarian team would collaborate on a script and a storyboard in a linear fashion. For GOTL, the creative process was more iterative. The team tried to match scenes from *Guardians of the Galaxy* with learning objectives but changed the ideas, movies scenes, and the lessons a few times before coming to a decision. However, once the team made a decision, the script was written quickly.

For each video, the team wanted viewers to identify with the characters, so a believable storyline was imperative. The overarching story for the entire GOTL series would find the protagonists assigned in a group for a research project, a situation all college students have experienced. The team found that watching parodies helped to find ways to take liberties with the storyline. The trailers and many parodies often used the most recognized song from the movie: "Hooked on a Feeling" by Mark James, sung by Blue Swede. The song is catchy, and it would be effective to parody this song for the first episodes.

The Song

First, the emerging technologies librarian and student worker collaborated on new lyrics for the song. Then the student worker asked her friend, a musical theater major, to sing it. He was wholly enthused to be a part of something outside of Rider University's musical theater program. He was told the background, the goals for the series, and where the song would be placed. He then read over the lyrics and made some small changes to enhance them. The final recording was a home run for the production team. The voice was very well done, and the song makes the entire project of higher quality.

> "I've got an assignment, it's due on Monday, I can't get to the library. I won't overdo it. I'll just google fu it. Then I'll probably just get a C."—Johnny Bernie

Casting the Characters

Casting was one of the first things that came to mind when envisioning Rider University's own take on *Guardians of the Galaxy*. To make this project feasible, the team looked within the library to find the cast. The following is a list of the main characters, the actors who portrayed them, and their connections to the GOTL project.

- **Peter Quill (Book Lord)**, the lead character, was played by the library systems manager (Dave), who was involved with the library's previous promotional videos series. He has a resemblance to the lead character in the movie and is great on camera. In the movie, this character calls himself "Star Lord," but the team decided to use "Book Lord" instead for a library connection.
- **ProQuest** was played by Hannah, a student worker who was thrilled to be offered the part. She also has a resemblance to Gamora from the movie. For the parody, she was named after a library database vendor (ProQuest). It was an inside library joke, but touches like these make the parody unique.
- **Rocket** was played by a librarian's three-year-old daughter. Though Rocket is male in *Guardians of the Galaxy*, the girl was a good fit for this GOTL role since Rocket is a two-foot-tall racoonlike character. Including a child in the video added an adorable factor and jokes, such as escaping from time out and coloring on the library walls.
- **Drax** was portrayed by the Moore Library's department chairperson, very involved in TRLM and a huge fan of the *Guardians of the Galaxy* movie. However, since department chairpersons are often busy, this character wore a mask so another person could fill in for future episodes if neces-

sary. Instead of referring to him as Drax the Destroyer, the team called him Drax the Dictionary Crusher.

- **Groot** was played by a plant and a figurine in the first two episodes of the series. Originally, a seven-foot-tall athlete agreed to perform as the tall treelike character, but schedule conflicts made it difficult for him to attend shoots. The team had to think creatively and work with what was available. These substitutes turned out to be satisfactory replacements in the videos.

Figure 4.1 shows the cast of the Guardians of the Library: ProQuest, Peter Quill, Drax, and in front, Rocket holding Groot.

Table Read and Scenes

The team took cues from show business for GOTL and invited the cast to a table read. The actors read through the script and offered suggestions for

Figure 4.1.   Cast of the Guardians of the Library.

revision. The team also wanted to make sure they were familiar with the scenes and plans.

The first episode was designed with two scenes. In the first scene, each character walks into the library slowly following one another, mimicking the trailer for the movie. The following scene imitates the scene in the movie where the officers discuss the background of each of the characters under arrest. This episode serves to introduce the series and the characters and pique students' interest. The second episode is loosely based on the prison-break scene from the movie. In the movie scene, the characters are planning how to escape, and the team felt this was an easy parallel to planning a group project.

Filming

A film and media studies major student taught the team some very important rules, such as taking three good takes of each scene and directing in a way that would make the editing more efficient. There are some artistic directions that cannot be taught, and when he was off the project, the team noticed the videos were not as well framed. Directing is an art that fortunately came naturally to the library student worker involved with GOTL.

When it came time to film and direct GOTL, the student worker took full ownership of the project. Having her serve as director was a strategic choice as she was primarily responsible for editing. The student worker could direct the shoot in a way to make the work easier on herself, filming as many takes and long shoots as she felt necessary. The video shoot took over two hours for the two episodes (one would be ninety seconds, and the other six minutes). The student worker had experience from a film production course in high school, where she learned how to organize and streamline the process. She explained her process as follows:

> I, as the sole director, knew the script really well and already envisioned how I wanted things to be set; I needed to make this project as easy and efficient as possible because we had a three-year-old with limited attention. I was able to film scenes in their entirety while speaking lines that would later be voiced over. I then knew where and how long each speaking part was for each character. I set the scenes so they would be easy for everyone to understand. Before filming, I had the cast meet. I wanted everyone to sit down and do a table read to help everyone walk through the vision. I made changes to small parts and added direction onto my script that was later updated for the cast. While filming, I did not just use the camera I was provided; I also used my iPhone. The iPhone really helped capture our opening scene in slow motion. I used what I had learned from my high school film class and applied it to the knowledge gained from making tutorials and episodes of TRLM. I can now say after the product has been finished, I did produce something that turned out very awesome.

This could only have been accomplished because the team decided to abide by some core principles: nothing is ever perfect, get out of the way of the student workers, and let the creativity fly high.

Voiceovers

When creating voiceovers for the lecture captures, the team found that using the flip camera instead of a typical computer headset to capture the narration ensured even audio quality with the captured film. For GOTL, the Rocket character was delivering the plan for the episode, but the preschool-aged actor could not perform the voiceover. It was suggested that the librarian would be best for the voiceover as she intrinsically knew what needed to be emphasized. Since Rocket is a male character, the librarian downloaded a voice-changing app on her android phone. The sound quality was fine, but the software sped up the narration in the process. A decision has not yet been made on how to proceed for future voiceovers. While the use of advanced audio software might work, the team has asked theater students to volunteer as voiceover talent. More students involved in the video would generate more interest from the student body.

Capturing the Library Lesson

The librarian was responsible for screen-capturing the library lesson piece of each video. She wrote the storyboard for the screen capture prior to filming and discussed it with the GOTL student workers to ensure the lesson was appropriate and understandable. One mistake the librarian made when creating the lesson for an episode of GOTL was not finalizing the full capture until after the film shoot. When creating the capture using TechSmith's Camtasia Studio, the librarian realized late she wanted to make changes to include another related learning objective. When the librarian presented the student worker with a screen capture that varied from the storyboard, the student worker found a way to make it work, but it was at the expense of a good joke.

Editing

Originally, the team thought an investment would need to be made in new equipment and software for video editing. When it was discovered that TechSmith's Camtasia Studio would be sufficient, the team was relieved not to have to purchase or learn any new software. However, with each new video produced, the team has considered upgrading the editing process and making use of the Apple computers and Final Cut Pro software available in the on-campus television studio. The team believed that videos in the Guardians of the Library series would really benefit from an upgrade in editing software, but it was difficult to find an available time in the studio as the semester progressed. The team made an effort to use a Windows-based movie editor instead, but the software products freely available seemed to be better suited to amateurs. The team relied on a few of the advanced features in Tech-Smith's Camtasia Studio, such as overlapping editable tracks, which is a must for adding callouts and pointers to information on the screen.

Copyright and Fair Use

While creating the informative promotional videos, the team made use of outside images, songs, or movies very occasionally. The preferred choices for nonoriginal media were items in the public domain or items with a Creative Commons license. The team also experimented with using popular copyrighted songs as a fair use exception. YouTube has a mechanism to protect its content creators and will send a dispute when there is a possible violation of copyright; therefore, it is important to place a fair use statement on the videos.

For the GOTL series, the team took more risks with copyrighted material. It was important for the library to set an example in terms of giving credit to the intellectual property of others. With the fair use exception of the Copyright Act, the team could argue the videos were educational, noncommercial, and transformative in nature. The parody would have no negative effect on the market for the original work. Parodies are considered a fair use, but it is advised to make a statement so it is very clear that this is a parody (Rich, 1999). As a library-sponsored project, the videos needed to err on the side of caution and be an example in terms of respecting copyright.

Video Hosting

The team hosted videos on YouTube and the RUL's LibGuides (Springshare) platform. It was important to us that all videos were accessible to those with hearing impairments. YouTube has tools that make the process of adding captions quite easy. YouTube is a platform with which students are very familiar, but LibGuides provided several additional benefits. LibGuides gave the videos an official presence on the rider.edu domain. LibGuides also enabled other librarians to reuse or link to any video in their own course or subject-specific research guides. The final benefit filled the emerging technologies librarian's overambitious goal to create a video on each possible topic or force as many learning objectives into one video as possible. With LibGuides, related content can be placed right next to each episode. Hopefully, after viewing the promotional videos, students are interested in clicking on the links to learn more.

PUBLICIZING THE SERIES

Since past efforts to publicize informative videos series were not effective enough by the team's own standards, a lot of planning was put into publicizing GOTL. The team wanted to build up excitement and promote the videos in the spring semester. Publicity efforts could start in advance of the release. The team created a website, T-shirts, and stickers for the series and held a preview party.

Merchandise

To increase hype prior to the release of the videos, the team created custom T-shirts and stickers and spent a lot of time designing these promotional materials to be very attractive. Many departments on campus give out free T-shirts; these needed to stand out. It was decided to create long-sleeve T-shirts to be more formal and different. Free Marvel-inspired fonts at fontspace.com and the CustomInk design tools were used to design the logo. The team developed three dozen different prototypes and got feedback from students and library staff before arriving at the final logo. The team aspired to highly professional-looking promotional materials. During the proofing process, the T-shirt vendor, CustomInk, called the team to discuss the possible copyright infringement of the T-shirts. However, when the librarian explained where the fonts were acquired and the purpose of the T-shirts, the customer service representative approved the design. The stickers were ordered from uPrint ing.com, and there was no question of copyright from their end. Both the T-shirts (see figure 4.2) and the stickers (see figure 4.3) acknowledge the older TRLM series and provide the URL to the GOTL website (http://guides.rider.edu/guardians). The budget allowed for a free T-shirt for each member of the library faculty and staff who would agree to wear the T-shirt on campus regularly.

The Preview Party

As a part of the promotional campaign for the series, the team organized a preview party. This preview party also served as an opportunity to pilot the first two episodes of the series and gather feedback. The preview party was held during finals week. Pizza and other snacks were provided. The last time the library held a free food event, a focus group, all of the attendees said that they visited the library three plus times a week. To prevent that inward discussion, the pair created fliers, posting only five in the library and giving ninety to the student worker to disperse on campus. The student worker created an event invite on her personal Facebook account, which gathered a lot of attention. The librarian created an ad on the library's Facebook page,

Figure 4.2. Guardians of the Library T-shirts were distributed to library staff and as prizes at the preview party.

which received no interaction. This is more evidence supporting student-librarian collaborations; the library may have had little success without the student's help. The preview party had more diversity in attendees compared to the previous focus group; of the students who attended the video promotion party, only seven visited the library three plus times per week, four said they visited one to two times per week, four answered one to three times per month, and one said it was his or her first time this semester.

The students were told to pay attention because they would be quizzed immediately after watching the videos in order to win one of the limited-edition T-shirts. They all wanted the T-shirts, which made the students focus on the lessons within the episodes. The questions students were asked to answer to win T-shirts were:

Figure 4.3. Guardians of the Library stickers were created to advertise the series across campus.

1. What database were they searching? Answer: Library One Search (Rider's discovery tool)
2. What was the group's research topic? Answer: Life on Other Planets
3. How did the narrator limit the searches? Three Answers: Full Text, Date, and Source Type
4. What was the name of the female character instead of Gamora? Answer: ProQuest

The winners were proud to receive their shirts, and all twenty-one students in attendance were also given GOTL stickers.

The students enjoyed the videos immensely. Their comments were that they were fun, funny, enjoyable, cute, cool, informative, witty, useful, and helpful. All but one student said they learned something from the videos, and there was a helpful suggestion to slow down the narration so the lesson could be easier to follow. All students stated they would watch more videos, but one did qualify it by writing "only if there was more free pizza!" This feedback gave reassurance that the videos would be appealing to the rest of the campus community.

The next steps in publicity will be to place ads in the campus newspaper and on the campus radio station for the start of the spring semester. Then we will place these videos online for the world and let them go viral, if they do.

MOVING FORWARD

The team plans to create more episodes, parody more from the movie's musical sound track, continually promote, and get more student participation. Most viewers find this project very exciting, and many students have stated they want to volunteer. There is a demand for the merchandise. At this point, the production team is achieving what they set out to do; there is a small buzz brewing on campus.

The team will focus on formally assessing the efforts as the project moves forward to learn what practices are worth the time and monetary investments. RUL expects to see a dramatic increase in view counts and students' self-reported perceptions of the library and its tools because of these promotional videos.

LESSONS LEARNED/BEST PRACTICES

For librarians attempting to create their own buzz on campus with promotional videos, the following advice is offered.

1. **Collaborate with students.** Today's college students have grown up interacting with media, adapt very quickly to the changing environment, and many have created and edited their own video content (Klapperstuck and Kearns, 2009). Student workers are essential to connecting with the younger generation. Not only do student workers help by taking on some of the more tedious editing work, but they make the videos relevant to today's college students. Marketing to college students is effective when an actual college student is there to validate or veto any of the librarian's ideas.
2. **Know your audience.** Think of what the audience would enjoy seeing. Constantly seek out that answer by previewing pieces of the episodes. Watch the viewers and note when they laugh and what they do not understand. Know your audience's frustrations with the library and the research process, and play on that in your videos.
3. **Let the creativity fly high.** Brainstorm silly, funny, odd, boring, and smart ideas. Rely on the creativity of others. Give the student worker an uncomfortable amount of creative control. Create a good, solid idea for a script or a song parody and then get out of the way—give the actors and your vocalist freedom to improvise.
4. **Take your time and plan.** The time spent on this project was far greater than anticipated. Moving slowly is very challenging for people who just want to be immediately productive. In the rush to move on to the filming and editing, it is important to remember to slow down and

fully develop the script and storyboard. Design, plan, and think it all out before the start of production. Taking the time to watch related videos on YouTube is not time wasted for it often sparks new ideas that can be used for the script, sequence, or editing.

5. **Realize that the primary purpose of promotional videos is to increase awareness.** These videos can and should be short. They are not meant to do all of the teaching and training done in a library. Do not be tempted to point out all of the different nuances of each library database. Promotional videos can positively impact students' perceptions of the library so that they see the library's relevance and usefulness to their work as college students.

6. **Don't be your own worst critic; nothing is ever perfect.** It is counterproductive to make everything flawless. There are some things you will not like in your videos, but you cannot remedy these without being inefficient. Your viewers will hardly notice the problems, and if they do, they forgive easily.

7. **Give credit where credit is due.** Cite the intellectual property of others. Do not forget that the rules apply for videos. Attribution is still necessary for works in the public domain or Creative Commons items found through Jamendo, Prelinger Archives, or CCmixter. Just like you tell students, cite what is not yours. In the same manner, give credit to all who assist in the process. Recognize that you could not have done it without a tremendous amount of support from the rest of the library and campus community.

CONCLUSION

Since librarians are already familiar with making tutorials, promotional videos are an achievable leap. The technology is becoming more accessible to use, and today's college students are much more accustomed to spending time watching videos online than ever before. The hardest part of creating promotional videos is discovering the creativity, but it can be found from people in the library. Librarians wishing to create their own promotional videos would do best to collaborate with students and give over a lot of creative control. At RUL, the emerging technologies librarian, with a lot of help from her student worker, switched from making informative videos to creating an exponentially more engaging series of promotional videos parodying one of the top-grossing movies of 2014. While creating the new series, the pair consciously created a campus buzz so that even before the episodes were released online, students on campus were talking about the videos and requesting the promotional materials. The time spent in creating the videos and the buzz improves the students' perception of the libraries and increases their likeliness to use the resources available to them.

REFERENCES

Babin, Zohar, Jordan Berman, and David P. Kronmiller. 2013. "What's On? How to Create and Curate Engaging Content!" Kaltura, November 14. http://corp.kaltura.com/webinar/whats-how-create-and-curate-engaging-content.

Glennie, Jennifer, and Tony Mays. 2013. "Rethinking Distance in an Era of Online Learning." *Internet Learning Journal* 2, no. 2: 127–43.

Hbllproduction. 2010. "New Spice | Study like a Scholar, Scholar." YouTube, July 15. http://youtu.be/2ArIj236UHs.

Klapperstuck, Karen J., and Amy J. Kearns. 2009. "The Wired Life: The Public and Private Spheres of the Gen M Community." In *Teaching Generation M: A Handbook for Librarians and Educators*, edited by Vibiana Bowman Cvetkovic and Robert J. Lackie, 111–24. New York: Neal Schuman Publishers.

Little, Geoffrey. 2011. "Managing Technology: The Revolution Will Be Streamed Online; Academic Libraries and Video." *Journal of Academic Librarianship* 37, no. 1: 70–72.

Lo, Leo S. 2011. "Design Your Library Video like a Hollywood Blockbuster: Using Screen-play Structure to Engage Viewers." *Indiana Libraries* 30, no. 1: 67–72.

Luo, Lili, Yuan Wang, and Lifeng Han. 2013. "Marketing via Social Media: A Case Study." *Library Hi Tech* 31, no. 3: 455–66.

Majekodunmi, Norda, and Kent Murnaghan. 2012. "'In Our Own Words': Creating Videos as Teaching and Learning Tools." *Partnership: The Canadian Journal of Library and Information Practice and Research* 7, no. 2: 1–12. https://journal.lib.uoguelph.ca/index.php/perj/article/view/2007/2618#.UqSzQfRDtqU.

Martin, Coleen Meyers. 2012. "One-Minute Video: Marketing Your Library to Faculty." *Reference Services Review* 40, no. 4: 589–600.

Mestre. Lori, S. 2012. "Student Preference for Tutorial Design: A Usability Study." *Reference Services Review* 40, no. 2: 258–76.

Nicholas, Martina, and Melba Tomeo. 2005. "Can You Hear Me Now? Communicating Library Services to Distance Education Students and Faculty." *Online Journal of Distance Learning Administration* 8, no. 2. http://www.westga.edu/~distance/ojdla/summer82/nicholas82.htm.

Oud, Joanne. 2009. "Guidelines for Effective Online Instruction Using Multimedia Screen-casts." *Reference Services Review* 37, no. 2: 164–77.

Perry, Anali Maughan. 2011. "Lights, Camera, Action! How to Produce a Library Minute." *College & Research Libraries News* 72, no. 5: 278–83. http://crlnews.highwire.org/content/72/5/278.full.

Rich, Lloyd L. 1999. "Parody: Fair Use or Copyright Infringement." Publishing Law Center. http://www.publaw.com/article/parody-fair-use-or-copyright-infringement/.

Saines, Sherri. 2011. "Circulation—the Making Of: Library Videos and the Real World." *Journal of Academic Librarianship* 37, no. 6: 532–35.

Schwartz, Meredith. 2012. "Texas A&M Libraries Film the Research Games." *Library Journal's Academic Newswire*, August 2. http://lj.libraryjournal.com/2012/08/academic-libraries/texas-am-libraries-film-the-research-games.

Thornton, David E., and Ebru Kaya. 2013. "All the World Wide Web's a Stage: Improving Students' Information Skills with Dramatic Video Tutorials." *Aslib Proceedings: New Information Perspectives* 65, no. 1: 73–87.

Wakiji, Eileen, and Joy Thomas. 1997. "MTV to the Rescue: Changing Library Attitudes through Video." *College & Research Libraries* 58, no. 3: 211–16.

Chapter Five

Promotion, Publicity, and Beyond

*Using a Marketing Plan and Innovative Strategies
to Reach Users in an
Academic Health Science Center Library*

Mary E. Edwards, Hannah F. Norton,
Michele R. Tennant, Nina C. Stoyan-Rosenzweig,
and Matthew Daley—University of Florida
Health Science Center Library

BACKGROUND

As medical libraries expand services and outreach efforts, there is a need for promotional and publicity activities to communicate value to the intended audiences. The University of Florida (UF) Health Science Center Library (HSCL) has developed various strategies to promote library services and activities, including the development of a marketing plan, leveraging existing resources, fostering external relationships, and encouraging innovative thinking. While the HSCL has marketed its services for years, it wasn't until relatively recently that a more comprehensive, planned approach was developed and implemented. As libraries find new ways to stay relevant in an ever-changing information landscape, librarians must adopt a culture of marketing to promote and publicize our value to users.

This chapter will describe the promotional and publicity efforts used by the HSCL and examine how the library identified the need and drafted a flexible plan for advertising to the university community and beyond. The chapter will also expand on innovative ways in which the library has implemented the marketing plan and promoted the library. It concludes with the lessons and best practices we learned about marketing and publicity from our varied experiences.

THE SETTING

The HSCL serves the Academic Health Center (AHC) at the University of Florida, which includes the Colleges of Dentistry, Medicine, Nursing, Pharmacy, Public Health and Health Professions, and Veterinary Medicine. While not physically located in the AHC, two related departments in the College of Health and Human Performance—Applied Physiology and Kinesiology; Health Education and Behavior—are also served by the HSCL. In addition to traditional reference and instruction services, we host a series of events featuring National Library of Medicine (NLM) traveling exhibitions, teach credit-bearing courses, offer new technologies such as 3D printing, provide information during patient rounds in the adjacent teaching hospital, and perform various outreach activities for time-limited projects. In order to promote our services and activities to users, the library developed a flexible marketing plan and has successfully used the plan to garner the attention of our audience.

The HSCL is part of the larger university library system known as the George A. Smathers Libraries. The system includes all the campus libraries excluding the Legal Information Center. While some of the HSCL operations are conducted by the Smathers Libraries (e.g., fiscal services and facilities), others including Web design and instruction are HSCL-specific. Often this works to the benefit of the HSCL because it can have tailored, dedicated personnel for key services and, when necessary, also utilize the resources and expertise of the larger system. For example, Smathers Libraries employs a director of communications who is responsible for activities like creating promotional material (printed posters, newsletters, bookmarks, and buttons), taking photographs for the website, and providing copy for press releases. While the HSCL has a staff member with dedicated marketing/Web responsibilities who assists with the creation of print and online materials, there are times when we can also receive promotional materials from the Smathers director of communications, allowing the library organization to leverage the expertise and resources of the larger system.

NEED FOR A MARKETING PLAN

Beginning in the fall of 2010, librarians at the HSCL decided to host traveling exhibits from the National Library of Medicine (NLM) more regularly and offer dedicated events in conjunction with these exhibits. The goals of having more events connected to the library were to bring people into our space, highlight research interests of faculty in the AHC, and do something new and creative as part of the broader campus community. Our first exhibit with expanded programming was *Rewriting the Book of Nature: Charles Darwin and the Rise of Evolutionary Theory*, and we hosted four related events: an opening reception, an informal talk over tea by a UF Darwin scholar, a Galapagos travelogue by a librarian, and a panel discussion by AHC students who participated in outreach trips in Central and South America. Despite interesting events that matched well with the exhibit and desired audience of AHC students and faculty, few people attended—fewer than twenty attendees at each event; fewer than ten at most (Auten et al., 2013).

This experience provided the impetus to develop a marketing plan that would ensure we were alerting the appropriate communities, on- and off-campus, of relevant events occurring at the HSCL. Because our users did not immediately consider the library a natural host for events, it was particularly important to communicate with them early and often about upcoming activities. With a newly expanded team of librarians (eleven in 2011 as compared to six in 2009) in the Biomedical and Health Information Services Department (previously known as the Reference Department), we expected to be introducing a variety of new services in addition to the exhibits and events. Developing a marketing plan helped clarify and make explicit existing methods that librarians were employing to keep users apprised of new services and materials; at the same time, creating the marketing plan encouraged librarians to brainstorm and explore new ways to reach users. The main goal in developing the marketing plan was to create a consistent but flexible process that anyone in the department could use to share news about the library with those who needed to know it—essentially, to demystify the advertising process.

EVOLUTION OF THE MARKETING PLAN

Although the marketing plan came about through the work of our small exhibits/events team, the entire department worked on its development, gathering contacts within their liaison groups and learning how to post information in AHC and campuswide newsletters, newspapers, and calendars. During the information-gathering stage of the marketing plan's development, our efforts were informed significantly by another ongoing project in which HSCL librarians were focusing on outreach: VIVO. VIVO (http://vivo web.org) is a semantic Web tool for generating and populating researcher profiles, designed to be used for researcher networking and collaboration. From 2009 to 2011, the University of Florida (along with six other institutions) was working on a National Institutes of Health–funded project to further develop this tool for national use, with librarians at HSCL and UF's

Marston Science Library involved in development, implementation, and outreach (Krafft et al., 2010). HSCL librarians were primarily involved in local outreach—informing researchers across campus about this tool, teaching them how their profiles would be updated, and encouraging their use of VIVO for finding interdisciplinary colleagues and potential collaborations. Through grant funding, the project was able to employ a dedicated marketing coordinator for both local- and national-level outreach. Working with the VIVO marketing coordinator helped our department identify several high-visibility venues for advertising: UF's employee website splash page, campus/hospital cafeterias and food courts, and hallway bulletin boards. The types of materials posted in these places included postcards, large-format posters, and table-top tents. VIVO outreach also relied substantially on in-person conversation with faculty and students through presentations at departmental meetings, the Faculty Senate sessions, campus research poster sessions, curriculum committee meetings, and deans' meetings. Although presentation at these meetings did not become part of the formal marketing plan, they were part of our overall strategy of communicating with users. One of the main lessons learned through VIVO outreach was that while the overall message needs to be consistent across the project, it should be customized to a particular audience.

The evolution of the HSCL exhibits/events program continued to impact the development of our marketing plan. In the spring of 2011, we hosted the next NLM exhibit, *Frankenstein: Penetrating the Secrets of Nature*, and nine accompanying events, including talks by three guest speakers from other universities, four film screenings, and two talks by UF faculty. Because several of these talks were interdisciplinary with a humanities focus, we successfully competed for funding from UF's Center for the Humanities and the Public Sphere (CHPS) to bring in some of the guest speakers. CHPS then advertised not only the events they had sponsored but also the entire series to their existing mailing list of contacts; they have become a permanent part of the marketing plan for events that overlap with the humanities.

Through the course of informing the CHPS about the details of our events and working to comply with their expectations about marketing, we received several helpful suggestions from their faculty about contacts within relevant departments as well as an unsolicited copy of their advertising contacts list. This four-page document was added to our existing marketing plan and significantly fleshed out details related to campuswide news venues and off-campus locations. As we continue to plan NLM exhibits and event series, a key element to brainstorming the types of events to hold has been searching the websites of other libraries who have hosted these exhibits. In addition to generating ideas for potential events, this has given us a better idea of the types of marketing materials, wording, and venues other libraries are using to

Harry Potter's World
RENAISSANCE SCIENCE, MAGIC, and MEDICINE

August 28-October 4 - Health Science Center Library
with additional events ongoing throughout the semester.

Learn more - http://guides.uflib.ufl.edu/harrypotter

Grand Opening
Thursday, Sept 6th
4:30-7pm
Health Science Center
Library, 1st floor

Harry Potter and the Sorcerer's Stone - Movie
Friday, September 7
6pm, Norman Gym
Contact nstoyan@ufl.edu
to reserve your seat

Representations of Race and Ethnicity in Rowling's Harry Potter Novels
Thursday, September 13
12-1pm, Communicore,
Room C1-7

Literary Alchemy: The Secret Magic Formula of Harry Potter and Today's Best-Selling Books
Wednesday, September 19
12-1pm, Communicore, Room C1-7

Modern Magic: Genetics in Medicine
Tuesday, September 25
12-1pm
Communicore, Room C1-7

Curses, Crimes, and Covenants: The Law and Harry Potter
Thursday, September 27
12-1pm, Smathers Library,
Room 1A

Harry Potter Magic at the Public Library
Sunday, September 30
1-5pm Alachua County
Public Library District
Headquarters

Potions and Herbs
Tuesday, October 2
12-1pm.
Communicore,
Room C1-7

Understanding Genetics: With a Little Help from Harry Potter & Friends
Wednesday, October 3
12-1pm
Communicore, Room C1-7

Harry Potter and the Deathly Hallows: Part 1 - Movie
Friday, October 26
5:30pm
Communicore, Room C1-4

Harry Potter and the Deathly Hallows: Part 2 - Movie
Tuesday, October 30
5:30pm
Communicore, Room C1-7

Figure 5.1. Harry Potter bookmarks promoting an activity in the series of events scheduled around the NLM exhibition *Harry Potter's World: Renaissance Science, Magic, and Medicine.* Matthew Daley.

advertise these exhibits. Figure 5.1 shows an example of marketing materials produced for one of our exhibits.

CURRENT MARKETING PLAN

The HSCL's current marketing plan is subdivided for three audiences: (1) members of the UF Academic Health Center, (2) all members of the UF community, and (3) the local community outside of campus. Promotion may take place to any or all of these groups based on the activity being marketed. For a full list of publicity venues used for each of the three audiences, see the appendix to this chapter.

Some of the events held at the library are primarily held for a specific subset (or the total) of the faculty, students, clinicians, researchers, and staff of the AHC. Such events might be stand-alone classes and workshops on databases or resources related to medicine or other health fields; vendor events, advertising, or training on similar products; or seminars or events related to health. In order to reach the members of the AHC without spamming everyone on the entire UF campus, a number of strategies have been developed:

- Sending e-mails to assigned liaison department and college listservs, and to the College of Medicine announcement list (monitored) (see figure 5.2 for an example)
- Posting information to the HSCL's website

- Adding slides to large display monitors hanging in the HSCL and around the AHC
- Contacting AHC News and Communications for potential publication in the *Post* (the monthly newsletter for the AHC) and *Insider* (online newsletter that publishes stories more frequently)
- Printing tabletop tents for the cafeteria and food court (needs permission)
- Printing posters to be placed in strategic buildings in the AHC (needs permission)
- Posting to HSCL social media sites—Facebook, Twitter, YouTube
- Contacting student groups in the AHC and asking for assistance in publicizing; contacting premed society
- Adding events to HSCL faculty and staff calendars

Many workshops, vendor demos, and events may be of interest to members of the UF main campus community as well; there are pockets of science-related students, faculty, and researchers throughout campus who may need a particular workshop, such as PubMed, or even nonscience people might be interested in an EndNote class or an exhibit on Harry Potter. In cases in which the team wants to promote events to the entire University of Florida, the AHC modes are used along with the following:

- Listing on the online University Calendar
- Listing on the online events calendar of the *Alligator* (the university newspaper)
- Posting a classified advertisement in the *Alligator* (selectively—there is a charge)
- Submitting stories to *Today* and *Florida* magazines (alumni association, well in advance)
- Sending to main campus library PR department for posting on library website, distribution to the library staff e-mail list, and potential inclusion in the Friends of the Library newsletter
- Creating a myUFL Portal Splash Page (scheduled more than a year in advance)
- Placing flyers in Reitz Student Union
- Sending flyers to the VA Library
- Announcing in the College of Liberal Arts and Sciences News
- Advertising in *GatorTimes* (UF undergraduate e-mail newsletter)
- Sending to non-AHC college publicity contacts, UF Honors college, deans, directors, department chairs, International Center, Center for the Humanities and the Public Sphere, UF retired faculty, and Provost's Office (faculty and postdoc weekly e-mail lists) for potential e-mail distribution

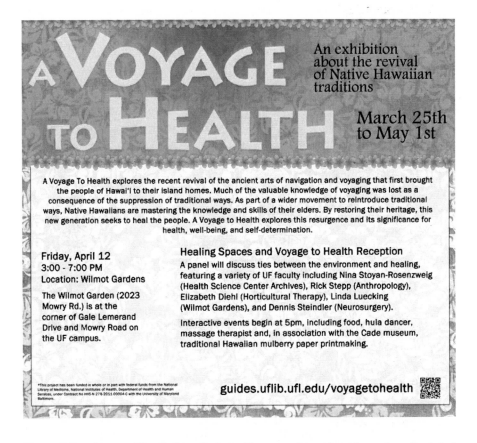

Figure 5.2. An e-mail invitation designed for one of a series of events scheduled around the NLM exhibition *A Voyage to Health*. Matthew Daley.

Some activities are so broad in their appeal that it makes sense to invite the entire Gainesville community. Such events have included the opening and events surrounding the HSCL's hosting of the National Library of Medicine's Harry Potter exhibits, as well as the annual conference of the UF Genetics Institute, an event that the HSCL cosponsored from 2005 to 2013. Advertising to those off campus includes the following venues:

- Electronic marquees at campus entrances (submit two weeks in advance)
- Local newspapers, TV stations, and newsletters
- Online calendar associated with local newspaper
- Civic Media Center
- County public library (posters and bookmarks)
- City website (communications office contact)

- Displays/bulletin boards at the local airport, grocery stores, and restaurants

There are a number of considerations required when advertising through the venues above. The first is that many have deadlines that are very early in the process, perhaps even before the details of our events are well formed. For example, posting on the splash page of the UF website can communicate to a wide number of students, faculty, and staff at the university, as the splash page is attached to the login for much of the business conducted at UF. However, this space is very popular and is often scheduled a year in advance. Thus it is important for the team to schedule as soon as the opening date for an NLM exhibit (for example) is known, even if no plans have yet been made for events related to the exhibit. Likewise, some publications only come out once or twice a year. One such publication is the Friends of the Library (main campus) newsletter, which is published only in November and June.

A useful marketing plan will not only list the outlets and their deadlines, but it will also provide a ready and current list of contacts for each of the outlets, including the preferred mode of contact. Any additional information, such as cost, preferred format for content, whether permission is required (and how it is granted), or other essential information should be included in the plan.

MARKETING MATERIALS

While an overall marketing plan is essential to ensure "big-picture" planning, there are enough variables with each specific outreach opportunity that you cannot always expect to create the same types of materials for each promotion and publicity campaign. To ensure the widest and most successful outreach, it is essential that the entire scope and potential reach of the service or program be explored before the marketing or promotional materials are created.

The HSCL employs a designer who is responsible for putting together the majority of in-house marketing materials; he is invited to the initial brainstorming session where the planning group meets to identify the best methods to promote the upcoming exhibit. Having a designer in-house is very useful as it allows the opportunity of free range of thought to construct a targeted plan. As with any marketing campaign, the promotional ideas are critical, but the implementation of those ideas into an aesthetically pleasing whole raises the visibility of the events and allows for a consistency of message and design across associated marketing materials. Furthermore, this consistency communicates and reinforces the library brand and increases the level of outreach and engagement with the university community and beyond.

Previous materials created to promote exhibits and events include two unique videos: one advertising a traveling exhibition on Harry Potter that featured a dementor flying outside the library doors; another advertising a campus humans vs. zombies event (Johnson et al., 2011; Norton et al., 2012), where a zombie was seen to turn from the library doors to look at the viewer. These are in addition to large-format posters that listed scheduled events, which were mounted to allow roving display on an easel in multiple areas; small promotional images on high-traffic university login user screens; physical bookmarks available from the service desks; e-mail announcements; exhibit labels; and more. Similarly, large-format posters have been created to advertise ongoing HSCL services and are displayed across the AHC; these are also reformatted and displayed electronically on large-screen monitors throughout the library and other AHC buildings. Figure 5.3 shows an example of marketing materials produced for one library service—our facility's research pods. Other services publicized by such posters include systematic reviews, literature searching, 3D printing, the liaison librarian program, HSCL stand-alone workshops, free interlibrary loan, and off-campus access, among others.

BEYOND THE MARKETING PLAN

The marketing plan was designed with a focus on venues that specifically advertise events. For developing and promoting other services and generating ideas for new services or events, relationships with centers, museums, and programs are also beneficial. These relationships provide meaningful ways to increase visibility, especially when they involve participation in or development of courses, lectures, events, and exhibits. Partnering with other university and community groups also helps to bring in new audiences, who may not know there is a medical library on campus, to raise the visibility of the library's offerings and—because of additional input and critique—to increase the value of offerings.

In particular, development of curriculum and courses helps to increase the audience's awareness of, interest in, and ultimately familiarity with library events. Of course, types of courses and the ability of librarians to participate in course development will vary from institution to institution, but it is well worth exploring all potentially available offerings. At the University of Florida, the honors program has a special course category—the (Un)Common Read (to distinguish from the Common Read, a program where every incoming freshman reads the same book), a series of one-credit undergraduate honors courses, each based on a single book. Courses to be offered each

Figure 5.3.   One of the posters promoting library services, designed to inform users about the various research software that HSCL provides. Matthew Daley.

semester are selected via proposal solicitations and vary from semester to semester and year to year, so a flexible program allows new and changing course offerings. The HSCL has been able to develop several courses to accompany NLM traveling exhibitions, including two sections (twenty-five students in each) to accompany the Harry Potter's World exhibit and one course to accompany *Voyage to Health*. In addition, the honors program and library are offering a course in the summer of 2015 on topics related to neurology and women's health. Students taking any of the courses are required to attend lectures and events. Some students even received credit for volunteering to teach at certain events and including that experience as part of their course project.

Other relationships have resulted in collaborative programs and exhibits that raised the visibility of the libraries. Professional teaching relationships established with the UF's Harn Museum of Art, for instance, morphed into collaborative projects that included tabling during a museum event on books—a table that focused on herbal medicines in nineteenth-century medical manuals and similar plants mentioned in Harry Potter's potions classes. This table helped to provide advance publicity for the Harry Potter exhibit. In addition, the archivist co-curated an exhibit on plant illustrations and use of plants in medicine. This exhibit included a number of activities, such as a gallery talk featuring the exhibit during museum family days and a Renaissance apothecary shop for a "Museum Nights" activity. The exhibit and visitor response became the focus of a specially designed survey, and the results were presented at a medical humanities conference. These partnerships, which sometimes occur outside of the library walls, also help to introduce the HSCL to audiences who might not be aware of its existence but who are then able to make use of our library's resources.

During the Harry Potter exhibit, the library partnered with the Alachua County Library District (local public library system) to create a small exhibit displayed for several months at the central library branch. We also moved the NLM traveling exhibition to the central library branch for a day, to accompany a day of science demonstrations there by staff from the Cade Museum of Innovation and Invention. In addition, the Cade Museum participated in a special event to accompany the *Voyage to Health* exhibit, drawing in participants who were familiar with the museum's activities.

The library has been able to partner with various AHC groups. One such group was the monthly History of Medicine lecture series, sponsored by a neurology faculty member and run by two second-year medical students. The series provides lunch and draws in a group of fifty or so students and faculty to each lecture. The lecture series organizers partnered with the library to provide a venue and lunch for two speakers who were part of the HSCL's lecture series on health issues during construction of the Panama Canal; attendance increased significantly. The Wilmot Gardens, a garden facility on campus that has been redeveloped as a healing garden near the hospital, provided a location and facilities for activities associated with the exhibit *Voyage to Health*, including a participatory hula dancing session from a local Hawaiian dance instructor. Finally, collaboration with faculty involved in the Local Global Health Equity Track—a curriculum innovation for medical students interested in developing special knowledge about work with the underserved—has provided additional audiences for the library's programs.

Although the collaborations and opportunities for working with the community and developing curricula will vary from library to library, they undoubtedly will exist in some form. A best-practices recommendation is that you take the time to develop relationships and learn about curriculum opportunities both within and outside your institution.

LESSONS LEARNED

Our experience in creating, implementing, and adapting a marketing plan to fit the needs of our users and leveraging existing relationships has taught us many lessons about promoting libraries. Therefore, we offer the following considerations for developing a marketing plan and creating engaging, successful promotions.

1. **Flexibility is key.** Any useful marketing plan needs to be flexible to adapt to the changing needs of the library, the differences in audience, and the variety of potential projects, resources, and events being promoted.
2. **Know your audience.** Although most of your services and programs will be designed for your primary users, understanding your community will help determine which services and events should be publicized to a broader audience.
3. **Customize to your audience.** While the overall message being conveyed should be consistent, customizing the specifics of the message (or the medium) for a particular audience helps ensure that varied audiences are receiving messages in a way that will produce the best response.
4. **Expand your audience.** Consider ways to bring in patrons who may not previously have known that the library existed.
5. **It's never too late to start.** Chances are you have been promoting your library in various ways for years. Now you can just begin to codify information about how you currently promote the library into a marketing plan.

6. **Leverage your resources.** If you have expertise and personnel available in a larger library system or elsewhere on campus, use these to supplement your promotion and marketing efforts.
7. **Be creative.** Find ways to develop coursework, events, and partners that may not be immediately apparent.

CONCLUSION

As libraries are competing with outside entities including coffee shops, bookstores, and the ubiquitous "Google search" to locate information, the need to promote their resources, services, and events becomes paramount. Marketing the library should be strategic and intentional, just as planning the library's mission, vision, and goals are strategic. Creating a marketing plan is the most efficient method to ensure a deliberate and effective means to promote library resources, services, and events. Once you have a plan, be prepared to think creatively about innovative ways to promote the library, including showcasing resources and expertise through community and curricular partnerships.

REFERENCES

Auten, Beth, Hannah F. Norton, Michele R. Tennant, Mary E. Edwards, Nina C. Stoyan-Rosenzweig, and Matthew Daley. 2013. "Using NLM Exhibits and Events to Engage Library Users and Reach the Community." *Medical References Services Quarterly* 32, no. 3 (July–September): 266–89.

Johnson, Margeaux, Melissa J. Clapp, Stacey R. Ewing, and Amy Buhler. 2011. "Building a Participatory Culture: Collaborating with Student Organizations for Twenty-First Century Library Instruction." *Collaborative Librarianship* 3, no. 1: 2–15.

Krafft, Dean B., Nicholas A. Cappadona, Brian Caruso, et al. 2010. "VIVO: Enabling National Networking of Scientists." Paper presented at WebSci10: Extending the Frontiers of Society On-Line, Raleigh, NC, April 26. http://journal.webscience.org/316/.

Norton, Hannah F., Beth Auten, Linda C. Butson, et al. 2012. "Zombie Pathology Lab: Using Health Information Resources during a Zombie Outbreak." Poster presented at the Quad Chapter Meeting of the Medical Library Association, Baltimore, MD, October 14. http://ufdc.ufl.edu/IR00001216/00001.

APPENDIX: HSCL MARKETING PLAN

Audience: AHC Only

1. E-mails to our departments and college listservs through library liaisons
2. HSCL website
3. TV monitors in HSCL and Communicore Building
4. *POST* (AHC monthly print newsletter)

5. Tabletops in Shands (hospital) cafeteria

6. Tabletops in Health Professions, Nursing, and Pharmacy Building (has open, cafeteria-like space)

7. Social networking sites

- HSCL Facebook page
- HSCL Twitter account
- HSCL YouTube
- HSCL Foursquare
- HSCL Yelp

8. Posters in AHC buildings: Communicore (where library and lecture halls are located); Health Professions, Nursing, and Pharmacy Building; Dental tower (of the hospital); Academic Research Building; Cancer/Genetics Building; Clinical & Translational Research Building; McKnight Brain Institute

9. Student groups

10. All-AHC List (moderated by the vice president for health affairs)

11. Outlook calendars of all HSCL staff

12. College of Medicine "Announce" listserv

Audience: All UF

1. University Calendar

2. *Alligator* (UF newspaper)

3. *Today* and *Florida* magazines (UF Alumni Association)

4. *Inside UF* (feed of top university news)

5. UF *News* (includes *Inside UF*, *Research News*, *UF in the News*, and other announcements)

6. myUFL Portal Splash Page (login page for campus finances, account management, time reporting, and other administrative services)

7. Updates on Smathers Libraries website

8. *Chapter One* (biannual Smathers Libraries print newsletter, sent to donors and friends)

9. Library News (web feed from Smathers Libraries)

10. Posters at the Reitz Union

11. Posters at the VA Library

12. College of Liberal Arts & Sciences News/Events

13. *UF Faculty Update* (weekly electronic newsletter)

14. *Gator Times* (weekly undergraduate electronic newsletter)

15. Search/e-mail student groups across campus

16. *Postdoctoral Update* (weekly electronic newsletter)

17. Posters or brief in-person announcements to UF retired faculty at monthly meeting

18. Other listservs for e-mail circulation:

- Honors program
- Deans, directors, department chairs
- International Center
- Center for the Humanities and the Public Sphere

19. Publicity contacts in the colleges = 16 total

Audience: UF + Public

1. Marquees at UF entrances

2. Public television and radio: WUFT 5 TV, WUFT FM, WUFT Community Update

3. *Gainesville Sun* (local newspaper)

4. Gainesville Calendar (calendar of *Gainesville Sun*)

5. *Gainesville Iguana* (local progressive newsletter and calendar of events)

6. *Fine Print* (local alternative, bimonthly publication)

7. Civic Media Center—posters, calendar, listserv

8. Gainesville Cultural Affairs—posters at recreational centers around Gainesville

9. Alachua County Library District—posters, blog

10. City of Gainesville Communications Office

11. Gainesville Airport—posters

12. Publix—bookmarks, posters at grocery store

13. Leave posters at other local businesses around town

Chapter Six

Branding for Relevance

A Public Library's Continuing Campaign for Access

Jessica Ford and Jim Staley — Mid-Continent
Public Library

BACKGROUND

In a time when e-books are changing the way people read, the perception that a library is merely rows and rows of books invokes the notion that the library is an institution of the past. Libraries are not the first established institution to face this challenge. With the rise of the Internet and twenty-four-hour news available through blogs and social media, newspapers have also endured a rough introduction into the twenty-first century. The main reason for this is that the newspaper industry held on to the idea that their product is the bundle that arrives on your doorstep and not the quality writing and reporting contained inside.

The lesson for libraries is that our institutions are not simply warehouses for books but the access point that provides entry into immeasurable amounts of information. As noted in OCLC's *Perceptions of Libraries, 2010: Context and Community*, "In 2005, most Americans (69%) said 'books' is the first thing that come to mind when thinking about the library. In 2010, even more, 75%, believe that the library brand is books" (De Rosa et al., 2011).

When Mid-Continent Public Library (MCPL), covering metropolitan Kansas City, Missouri, surveyed its customers, the story was the same. When asked, "What word best describes the library to you?" the answer given by almost 65 percent of the customers was "books/reading." MCPL, which was spending the third most money in the United States on total electronic materials (Public Library Association, 2011), was still thought of as a warehouse for books. Is it any wonder that despite thirty traditional branches, four automated locations, a special library dedicated to genealogy, a robust collection within the digital branch, and significant growth throughout the first decade of the 2000s, staff were still being asked whether the library would be around in the future?

Putting that question to rest became MCPL's primary goal as rebranding discussions began in 2011. First and foremost, MCPL wanted to move the public's perception of the library as a warehouse of books to a new understanding of the library as a place where ideas are shared and imagination is stimulated. A secondary, complementary goal was to use that new perception to educate customers about nontraditional library services and increase their use and value. To do that, the new brand needed to find a simple message that could both broaden the public's view of library offerings and communicate MCPL's true essence.

Everything has a brand. Businesses, organizations, and even people have a brand. Every interaction people have with an institution builds its brand. Yet, too often, branding efforts begin and end with a marketing campaign and never become part of the organizational culture. To create a fully pervasive brand, MCPL wanted to determine a central idea that could be used as the animating idea not just in marketing, but throughout the entire organizational structure.

MCPL needed to find a brand that represented what the public library was, as well as what *this* specific library stood for. The MCPL team looked both inside and outside of the library organization, searching for a concept that was both familiar to modern audiences and representative of the mission of the library. A survey of services was also done to determine common factors in those sometimes disparate offerings. And, finally, a thorough examination of the history of the MCPL system was used to determine what implicit brand decisions had been made over the years.

Best Practices

Don't think of branding as a marketing campaign. Good branding means tapping into and expressing what your organization is truly about.

FINDING FOCUS

Throughout the research process, the concept of "access" kept surfacing when the discussion turned to what libraries truly offer. As such, through focus groups and staff discussions, it was discovered that the idea of access not only gets at the root of what libraries do, but also begins to tie together the wide variety of products and services MCPL offers. Access is what keeps the library relevant, and what makes the library one of our country's most democratic institutions. It is why users can be educated, entertained, enhanced, and engaged just by walking through the door or logging on. Libraries represent opportunity, and access is the avenue by which that opportunity travels. Books, movies, music, tutoring, classes, events, and digital resources are all things to be obtained or experienced at a library, but it is the access to all of these that makes a library invaluable to any community.

In addition, access is an idea that has empowered MCPL since its inception. When individual library systems and voters from three separate counties came together five decades ago to create MCPL, the reason was to provide a level of access none could provide on their own. When the library system undertook a major building campaign in the 1980s and 1990s, the goal was to provide access to communities that previously had no access. And, in the early twenty-first century, MCPL began working on a project to put smaller, automated libraries in places where citizens already conducted their daily lives. The goal was to provide access.

Obviously, this all was pushing the library system in a very clear but challenging direction. Moving the public perception to the thought that libraries provide access and not books is a difficult proposition. Overcoming the deeply ingrained belief that libraries provide a quiet study area and a stack of books is one that would have to be carefully deconstructed and rebuilt, not around the container, but the content. Library users and non-users alike needed to be reminded that libraries are portals for ideas and not books on a shelf. More broadly, it required a change in focus from libraries as places to an access point that provides information to a variety of media, which *can* include physical places.

But branding is much more than building a promotional message. Brands are not what a company says they are; they are what a company really *is*. Access is who MCPL *is*. As discussed previously, it was what MCPL has always been. Rebranding is then, really, about consciously claiming what the organization has always been about and focusing on the concept in organizational decision making and daily operations. It means staff knowing that access is the primary purpose of the library and taking pride in providing the best access possible. It means MCPL board members advocating on behalf of the library with the purpose of increasing access. And it means customers expecting, receiving, and recognizing the value of great access.

MCPL, which turns fifty years old in 2015, will continue to put a major emphasis on ensuring access to resources that educate, entertain, and enrich our citizens and community; again, access is what MCPL is all about, and it is this concept that inspires and informs the MCPL's branding statement:

Access is not only the principle on which the Library was founded, but continues to be our primary aspiration today and in the future. Access is the reason MCPL continues to outpace other libraries in budgets allocated for materials. When a user cannot find an item on branch shelves, the Library will work with any of its 9,100 partner institutions to locate and retrieve it at no cost because we value access. MCPL supplies users with online resources unparalleled in the Midwest, and access is why. The Library is quickly expanding eBook offerings because of access. Tutors are available 84 hours a week for students. Teachers can request books for their entire classroom. Small businesses can receive demonstrations of library resources. Anyone can attend educational and entertaining programming at any of our 30 branches. All of these are direct results of a singular focus on access. (Staley, 2011)

Of course, a good brand message is also needed to carry the idea to the public and focus the staff. The brand message and campaign would need to be focused, clear, flexible, and sustainable. It would also need to communicate with various groups of stakeholders. A specific message was needed for each stakeholder group; some individuals would receive several of these messages since they might be part of multiple stakeholder groups. The sidebar shows the groups identified and the takeaway message for each.

Stakeholder Groups and Messages

Stakeholder	*Message*
Community members	Libraries aren't just books.
Noncustomers	The library has services that will improve your life.
Customers	We have more to offer you.
Community leaders	The library remains as relevant as ever.

Because the access brand was working against such an ingrained idea, the marketing team decided to avoid a simple tagline that could end up fading into the background. Instead, MCPL developed a layered tag message. This system consists of a base message and a series of secondary messages. The base message was designed to communicate the brand in the broadest terms. The secondary messages apply that brand proposition to specific target audiences and library services. The subtle changes in the layered messages require the reader to consciously engage the language in a way that simple taglines do not.

Each message was carefully crafted to appeal to the selected audience in a targeted way. Before our rebranding, when the marketing team created messages, the focus was on what MCPL offers customers. The rebranding changed the way of thinking to start asking the question, "How do our services and products affect customer access?" This was reflected in the language chosen as well as in the design. The desire was for the language to be presented in easy-to-understand messages and paired with an easy-to-follow design.

The base message developed for this campaign was "Access Your World" (see figure 6.1). This message communicates the brand essence of access, implies wide-ranging service offerings, and is a call to action. The base message is used any time MCPL is promoted in the broadest terms and to the broadest audiences. In this sense, it can function as the tagline of the library.

However, "Access Your World" does not appear regularly in MCPL communications. Instead, most communications carry a secondary message that applies the brand message in a more targeted way. Figure 6.2 illustrates some examples of library product advertisements and the accompanying access message.

Like the primary message, the secondary messages focus on a benefit for the customer. In the case of job search resources, the message doesn't focus on research databases or résumé assistance but instead on the opportunity that comes with new employment. The idea that remains present in each application is that of access. As the audience encounters multiple messages,

Access Ideas
Access Imagination
Access Community
Access Opportunity
Access Your World

MID-CONTINENT
PUBLIC LIBRARY

Figure 6.1. Access Your World.

Figure 6.2. Access Messages.

the idea that there is much to access at the library builds. Artistically, the distinction between the consistent word—"Access"—and the variable words is maintained by the color scheme. The word "access" is consistently printed in either black or white, while the variable portion appears in a variety of colors.

An important choice made in the rebranding process was not to change MCPL's traditional "book" logo. While this may seem counterintuitive when the rebranding was attempting to change the image of the library away from books, the marketing team felt that it was critical that the rebranding process not become an exercise in changing the logo. Logo changes often take center stage in rebranding processes and obscure the fundamental organizational changes that are necessary to truly rebrand. The campaign relied on board member support, staff buy-in, and customer recognition, not opinions about new fonts and colors. In the access program, the logo will remain the same but, whenever possible, will appear with an access message.

Best Practices

Don't let your rebranding process become an exercise in changing the logo.

STAKEHOLDER ENDORSEMENT

The most important element to any rebranding effort is stakeholder engagement and endorsement. Before even considering external stakeholders, MCPL focused on the two main groups of internal stakeholders: the board of trustees and the staff.

Library Board of Trustees: Education and Ownership

In order for the new brand to permeate the entire organization, it needed ownership from the highest levels of the institution. MCPL's twelve-member board of trustees sets the direction for the library system's values, policies, and planning. Without getting the board to fully support the concept of "Access," MCPL would not be able to successfully implement the new branding.

An engaged and supportive board is critical to ensuring the organizational change necessary to rebrand. The MCPL board of trustees is made up of a diverse group of community members from a large tri-county area. As board members have varying degrees of interest and knowledge of branding, they were offered an overall session focusing on the basic concepts of branding and the importance of developing a brand. The presentation then explained the "Access" idea. While the framework of providing access was not new to the organization, the new brand required a change in language from, "The library provides information," to "The library provides access to information." This subtle rewording of MCPL's leadership's internal thought process gained resonance with the board. They adopted the brand concept immediately and began the process of organizational change.

Staff Training: Understanding and Vision

The next step in MCPL's organizational transformation was ensuring that the staff understood and bought into the message. To take that step, managers of branches and departments, as well as administrative leaders, participated in a specialized workshop that took them through the vision behind the new brand and the changes that the branding would bring to the organization. The goal was not only to educate them on the importance of having a brand, but also to illustrate that the work they were doing every day was already a part of creating an "Access" organization.

Best Practices

Change starts from within. Without taking the time to listen to and involve staff of all levels in large-scale organizational changes, a brand strategy will never be completely successful.

Frontline staff members attended a half-day coaching session called "AC-CESSability" training. The goal was to relay the concepts behind the new branding to the eight hundred staff members while explaining the importance of word-of-mouth marketing in expanding customer knowledge and promoting access to customers. Part of the motivation was to inspire ownership of the access brand in all of our staff members. No library can function without its staff, and at MCPL, as at all libraries, the frontline staff are the backbone of the entire organization and the best promotional resource for a new brand.

By focusing on the most important resource first, ther staff, the branding was able to begin from the inside out. Gaining the support from internal stakeholders allowed the access message to push beyond a marketing strategy to create the impetus for a complete organizational shift.

Becoming an Access Organization

As any good branding effort should, the idea of access has pervaded nearly every effort of MCPL. In 2012, just after the initial staff rebranding education took place, MCPL began the process of updating the strategic plan. Due to a systemwide dedication to access, the strategic plan process this time was remarkably different than ever before. The central question throughout the library's strategic planning process was, "How does this (the subject under consideration) affect access?"

Beginning with updating MCPL's mission statement, branding focus continued away from the services provided to what could be done to break down barriers to access. The previous mission statement was, "MCPL will provide exceptional customer service and expanding access to materials, programs, and technology, including a World Class Genealogy and Family History Library." You will notice that even before branding around access, the mission statement also contained the word "access." It really is who MCPL *is*! But this statement was really focused on the stuff done and the containers that the offerings came in. MCPL's new mission statement shifts to reflect a belief in the power of access—not just services and information but the powerful messages that unparalleled access can provide. The new mission statement is, "Mid-Continent Public Library's mission is to enrich our citizens and communities through expanding access to innovation, information, ideas, and inspiration."

As MCPL began the strategic plan process, the focus continued to be access. Instead of a strategic plan with eighteen different strategic directions focusing on our main organizational issues, the decision was made to simplify the plan and create a focused, clear, flexible, and sustainable strategic plan, based on the principles laid out in Sandra Nelson's *Strategic Planning for Results* (2008). Focusing on six goals that spanned all levels of the organization, MCPL's strategic plan was rewritten as follows:

1. Children from birth to age eleven will have programs and materials that stimulate their imaginations and prepare them to read at grade level.

2. Adults and teens will enjoy materials and programs in current and emerging formats that enhance their lives.
3. Adults and teens will have resources and programs that enable them to make informed decisions about health, wealth, and civic engagement.
4. Adults and teens will have the services and support they need to express themselves by creating original content.
5. Residents and visitors will have designated and welcoming spaces in which to meet and interact with others, connect to the digital world, or enjoy a quiet place.
6. Residents and visitors will have the resources they need to connect the past with the present through their family histories. (Mid-Continent Public Library, 2013: 1)

This change in the underlying strategy of the entire organization provides fertile groundwork for anything and everything MCPL does. By creating a focused plan with multiple measureable key performance indicators for each goal, MCPL created a comprehensive blueprint for a sustainable access-based organization.

Best Practices

Look for ways to implement the brand in unlikely places. Instead of only focusing your brand outside of the organization, consider using your brand to prompt changes in departmental procedures, evaluation techniques, or even strategic planning.

EFFECT ON INSTITUTIONAL VALUES

Since MCPL's strategic plan was initiated and approved in 2013, the organization has undergone a number of systematic and systemwide changes. MCPL discovered that when it is about access, it isn't about outputs, things, or buildings—instead, it is about becoming a vital part of the community and helping people obtain the resources that they need. Access is about providing service—where they want it, when they want it, and how they want it. And so the focus became content, not location.

In order to provide the support the library branches needed to become access points for their separate communities, MCPL's new strategies put access into practice. This was done by providing in-house support through various departments, putting more importance on community outreach, and working with the entire organization to provide ongoing measurable evaluation tools.

There is no department that has not been touched by the access brand. The access brand has fully saturated MCPL, most noticeably in the renaming of the frontline staff position from "library assistant" to "access specialist." The idea of access is constantly used to expand digital offerings through new resources and access points as well as to provide more educational opportunities for staff to be able to fully understand and communicate the importance of these nontraditional library services.

MCPL's Electronic Resources Department and Information and Readers Services Department are constantly working together to provide reference classes as more of our print resources are converted to electronic media. By creating staff practice questions and database training kits, as well as utilizing vendor webinars, they are not simply expanding our digital offerings—they are building a workforce that truly understands and promotes these resources effectively to their individual communities.

Best Practices

With full branding support on all levels, the institution should begin to see the benefit of continuing a brand through every department, position, and activity of the organization.

PUBLIC ROLLOUT

Taking the new branding out to the various stakeholder groups required an approach that used both traditional and new media tactics, both inside and outside the library. To measure the success of the branding efforts, the marketing team decided to look at three variables: stakeholder receptivity to the brand, use statistics for services promoted directly in the campaign, and media performance (impressions). The cost of the initial campaign was $164,200. Of that total, $75,000 came from direct library expenditures on media and printing, $70,000 represented staff time, and $19,200 was in-kind advertising support.

Internal Collateral

Access Pass

Library cards are one of the most cherished possessions of many library customers, and also one that is most associated with carrying books out of the building. MCPL renamed library cards "access passes" to highlight the idea that the card is a key to all that the library offers. These cards have been well received, and for many, they have become the visual focal point of the rebranding effort.

Access Guides

Live programming guides were also in need of a new direction. They were renamed "access guides" and supported that idea by grouping branches within the guides to expand customer usage of multiple branches. These guides were one of the primary elements that showcased the new branding design with ample white space and simple text formatting.

Access-ories

All MCPL staff received "Access Specialist" T-shirts, and all promotional items began carrying an Access message (figure 6.3). These included everything from coffee mugs to temporary tattoos for kids.

Public Relations

As part of the Access branding public relations strategy, journalists were educated on the importance of access to information by pitching alternative library service ideas and encouraging library spokespeople to work the word "access" into any broadcast recording or media conversation. Media specialists even started counting the number of times the library director said "access" in his speeches and to the media.

Figure 6.3. Accessories.

As a piece of the branding campaign, an emphasis was placed on increasing access to the library for the community through social media efforts. This meant not only adding the visual brand elements, but also increasing the contact and interaction within Facebook, Twitter, and other social media avenues.

MCPL's online library, app, and e-mail newsletter were all updated with the Access branding. In addition to design tweaks, staff pushed forward the brand elements of openness and clarity by emphasizing constant communication and interaction. The library director was also moved front and center and gave customers the opportunity to communicate directly with him via the website.

Advertising

Billboards, online media, and local television (see figure 6.4) were all incorporated to push the message outside the traditional library audience. Each medium received a series of ads that individually informed citizens about "wow factor" library services and, in total, conveyed the breadth of what can be accessed at MCPL.

Best Practices

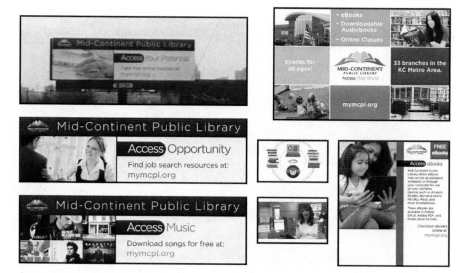

Figure 6.4.   Advertising.

Remember that every element of the organization can, and should, convey the brand.

EVALUATION

The primary brand push came to a close in early December 2012. The success of the effort was measured in three ways: media performance, use statistics for services promoted directly in the campaign, and stakeholder receptivity to the brand.

Media performance was measured in several ways. Quantitatively, both total impressions and unique impressions were measured across the collective media. Total impressions were 15 million across print, radio, television, and billboard buys. Unique impressions were over 3.4 million. With the variety of media, targeted demographic groups, and geographies, there is a high probability of having reached a very large percentage of residents in the MCPL service area. Among customers, frequency numbers were bolstered by the ability to place the message on all library promotional materials and online vehicles.

Several services received focus during the branding campaign. These services all saw significant growth during the period they were featured in the campaign. Circulation of e-books grew 191 percent over the same period the previous year. Use of online job search resources grew by 48 percent over the same period the previous year. Online tutoring sessions increased 37 percent over the same period the previous year. Two new services that were promoted had a direct increase during their campaigns. Enrollment in online classes grew by 23 percent, and music downloads grew by 227 percent!

The final quantitative number used for measurement is the percentage of customers who identify "books" as the word most associated with libraries, versus the percentage who put "access" in that spot. The follow-up to MCPL's previous survey took place in May 2013. Results show a 17.9 percent increase in the percent of people who said the word "access" best describes the library.

Qualitatively, multiple groups of stakeholders responded well to the campaign. Customers have enjoyed their new "access passes" and have made regular comments about the things they never knew the library did before. Multiple community leaders and elected officials have told MCPL that they believe the campaign really shows the true value of library resources. And staff have responded very enthusiastically, saying they are proud to be thought of as providers of access to resources that change lives. The greater library community has responded positively as well. MCPL's efforts around access and e-books were recognized by OverDrive (a global distributor of e-books), and MCPL staff have presented to multiple library groups around the country on the campaign.

In 2013, MCPL was selected as a winner of the John Cotton Dana Library Public Relations Award. In 2014, MCPL received the greatest award yet, the National Medal from the Institute of Museum and Library Services. Awarded specifically for a focus on literacy initiatives, making substantial collection and digital resource investments, and working with local and national partners to actively engage community members, this award showed that our branding campaign made an impact not only on the community but also on the library community as a whole.

At the end of 2014, Mid-Continent Public Library continued with its efforts to shift the public perception of the library from that of a dusty old building filled with hardbacks to that of the library as a great resource for quality information, no matter the format. The trick will be to remain relevant because the community remembers that what we truly offer is information and imagination. Those are offerings unlikely to go out of style anytime soon.

REFERENCES

De Rosa, C., J. Cantrell, M. Carlson, P. Gallagher, J. Hawk, and C. Sturtz. 2011. *Perceptions of Libraries, 2010: Context and Community*. OCLC. http://www.oclc.org/reports/2010percep tions.en.html.
Mid-Continent Public Library. 2013. "MCPL Strategic Planning Goals." Paper presented at the Mid-Continent Public Library Board of Trustees Meeting, Independence, MO, February.
Nelson, Sandra S. 2008. *Strategic Planning for Results*. Chicago: American Library Association.
Public Library Association. 2011. *Statistical Report*. Chicago: Public Library Association.
Staley, James. 2011. "Mid-Continent Public Library Brand Statement—Access." Paper presented to Mid-Continent Public Library Administrative Team Meeting, Independence, MO, January.

Chapter Seven

People Do Still Read E-mail!

E-mail Marketing as an Academic Library Outreach Tool

Jamie Hazlitt — William H. Hannon Library,
Loyola Marymount University

WHY E-MAIL MARKETING?

How much "junk" e-mail do you receive in your inbox daily? How many messages do you delete without reading, even though they come from companies or institutions from whom you signed up to receive regular communication? When considering the amount of e-clutter that comes into our lives— and those of library users—on a daily basis, it may seem counterintuitive or even futile to add your library's messaging into the mix. But research in the corporate marketing world continues to affirm e-mail marketing as a powerful tool for driving customer engagement (Aufreiter, Boudet, and Weng, 2014). What can libraries learn from the corporate world's approach to e-mail communication? Does e-mail marketing have a place in a library communication strategy? At the William H. Hannon Library at Loyola Marymount University, the answer to this question is a resounding yes.

TIME FOR CHANGE

In 2009, Loyola Marymount University (LMU)—a premier Catholic university in West Los Angeles serving 6,000 undergraduates, 2,200 graduate students, and 1,200 law students—celebrated the grand opening of the new William H. Hannon Library. Architecturally stunning, centrally located on campus, and situated on a bluff with 270-degree views across the city from the Pacific Ocean to Hollywood, the new library building was undoubtedly an attention getter. In the year leading up to the opening of the new library, the dean of the library assigned a working group to develop a communication plan to keep the campus informed of updates related to the new building and the complex task of moving an entire library from one building to another. Prior to the formation of this group, library communication efforts—which included writing on a whiteboard, one-to-one communication between librarians and faculty, and the occasional flyer—had limited reach beyond the walls of the old Von der Ahe Library.

The first task of the newly formed communication team was to launch a library blog, which provided the library with a cost-effective and user-friendly platform to update the community about the move. Librarians selected Typepad as the vendor for the blog, tweaked a premade template to customize the blog's appearance, and started publishing. The blog content emphasized the visual, adopted a casual, approachable voice, and aimed to balance the informative with the entertaining. Users could access *Hannon Library News Blog* content through an RSS feed on the library home page. Hannon Library also had some early success with its Facebook "fan page" and frequently used this as another avenue to cross-post blog content. But the biggest challenge with the news blog in 2009 was the same challenge faced today: attracting readers.

During the first year in the new William H. Hannon Library, over 750,000 visitors came through the doors. Over the course of the year, the library programming committee designed an ambitious lineup of programs—author visits, films, faculty speaker series, and traveling exhibitions—that far surpassed anything attempted previously in the old library. Program attendance was small but enthusiastic. During this time, the blog was still the library's primary source of online publicity—but through anecdotal feedback throughout the year, librarians heard a common refrain: "I didn't know the library was doing all of this stuff!" With blog posts averaging only sixty views each (a paltry percentage of our users) in 2009–2010, librarians concluded that the blog was not having the desired impact and began to diversify their communication efforts.

HAPPENINGS @ HANNON

In the summer of 2010, an expanded library communication team (chaired by the new outreach and communication librarian, with membership including librarians and library assistants) made a strategic decision to expand methods of communicating with the LMU community. Librarians reached out to the university's Office of Communication and Government Relations to establish workflows for more consistent integration of library content into LMU's central communication channels. In the interest of "being where the users are," the library continued to build its Facebook following through contests and incentives and had some success with expanded reach there. The @lmu-library Twitter account was launched, and the library communication team started to research and apply social media content best practices, developing internal social media policies and procedures to provide structure to these new modes of communication. But this was not enough.

Librarians expressed concerns about reaching users who opt not to use social media, or who do but choose not to "follow" the library. And even though the LMU library Facebook and Twitter accounts collectively had thousands of followers, the communication team was also concerned about library content getting "lost" in the endless streams of social media content—so that users who presumably opted to follow the library may not even see what we are publishing. Inspired by the newsletters highlighted at the 2010 American Library Association's annual conference program PR XChange, the communication team decided to pilot a monthly e-newsletter—and *Happenings @ Hannon* was born. In the following section, you will learn about the decisions made and steps that needed to be taken before publishing the first issue; how librarians developed and continue to grow the mailing list, the resources, and the workflows needed to publish regularly; and how the impact of *Happenings @ Hannon* and its value for the LMU community is assessed. The chapter concludes with ideas for the future evolution of Hannon Library's own e-mail communication strategy. Integrated throughout, you will find suggestions and best practices for librarians considering launching their own periodical e-newsletter.

Selecting a Vendor

At its most basic level, an e-newsletter could simply be sent out to an existing mailing list as a PDF attached or embedded through Microsoft Outlook or another enterprise e-mail system. But the William H. Hannon Library communication team found the idea of a full-service e-mail marketing vendor appealing, as these companies offer robust solutions for managing mailing lists, designing and customizing e-mail templates, keeping detailed statistics, providing marketing support, integrating with social media, hosting media content, archiving e-mails, and more. (In other words, much more than the library had the capacity to do with existing resources in-house!) For most full-service e-mail marketing services, pricing is determined on a sliding scale depending on the number of subscribers on your mailing list—ranging from free for under two thousand subscribers to two hundred dollars a month for more than twenty-five thousand subscribers. After exploring a few different vendor options, the decision was ultimately made to subscribe to Constant Contact because their selection of templates was appealing, their pricing was competitive (especially with a discount for nonprofit organizations), and their back-end content creation and mailing list management system appeared to be intuitive and user-friendly. Constant Contact also offers regular training and professional development opportunities for their clients, and over the years, the Hannon Library communication team has found their customer service to be excellent. Although Constant Contact has been a first-rate choice for the William H. Hannon Library, we recommend that libraries considering outsourcing e-newsletter content management explore as many options as possible to find a vendor that is the best fit for their institution.

> Compare features and pricing from a number of vendors before deciding what the best solution for your institution might be. The following companies are great places to start:
>
> - AWeber (http://www.aweber.com)
> - Constant Contact (http://www.constantcontact.com)
> - Emma Mail (http://myemma.com)
> - iContact (http://www.icontact.com)
> - MailChimp (http://mailchimp.com/)

Identifying Our Audience

Happenings @ Hannon was launched as a general-purpose library newsletter—intended to cast as wide a net as possible across all users of the library at LMU and provide a monthly snapshot of upcoming programs, services, and featured collections or resources. This was an ambitious undertaking, and although e-mail marketing best practices often prescribe more granular segmentation of target audiences, this was a deliberate decision about the e-newsletter audience based on the internal human resources dedicated to communication. Libraries with one or more full-time professionals dedicated to communications might be well served to create a suite of custom e-mail newsletters with content tailored to specific audiences. But for Hannon Library, with one librarian fully responsible for communication as only a portion of her responsibilities, starting with a single e-newsletter for the entire community at large made the most sense.

Although the decision was made to create a single newsletter with a broad reach, the librarians at LMU did not ignore targeted communication altogether. For student and parent outreach, they sought out opportunities to disseminate library information through partners on campus with more direct access to these individual user groups than the library. For example, twice annually, the library placed a column in the e-newsletter sent from the Parent Programs Office to the parents of first-year undergraduates, and information of interest to graduate students was periodically sent to the Graduate Student Association of LMU, who then featured this library news in their own social media. The LMU Department of Community Relations helped promote the library's public programs off campus with a reach that the library would not have otherwise. In the future, the library communication team also plans to explore more targeted e-mail communication directly from the library to donors and faculty.

Building Our Mailing List

Considering the broad target audience described above, the library was faced with the question: "How do we reach 'everyone'?" Like many academic institutions, LMU has a university anti-spam policy that prohibits individual units—including the library—from sending out all-campus e-mail communication. The library communication team also wanted to follow e-mail marketing best practices, which prescribe an opt-in method of building a mailing list. From the first issue on, it was important to ensure that everyone who received *Happenings @ Hannon* in their inbox was doing so because they explicitly asked for communication from the library. So how could they make this happen?

The communication team decided to start with what they already had. For the first issue, the librarians created a "starter" mailing list of approximately nine hundred individuals who had opted to receive library communication in one form or another over the previous two years. This included library donors, workshop attendees, faculty liaisons, and visitors who signed exhibition guest books and included their e-mail address. But students were notably absent from this list! To address this, before launching the first issue, librarians and staff hosted a "Happy Birthday Hannon" party outside the library during the first week of class. Passersby were invited to have a slice of cake, sign an oversized birthday card, and in exchange for signing up for the library's brand-new e-newsletter, they were entered into a drawing for a fifty-dollar campus dining gift card. At the end of the birthday party, the library's mailing list had grown from 900 to 1,100, and the library communication team was ready to send out the first issue of *Happenings @ Hannon*.

Over the past five years, the library has implemented the following strategies to continue to grow its newsletter subscription base:

- Sign-up sheets, placed at every service desk in the library, are processed and refreshed on a regular basis.
- Sign-up sheets are taken to every library outreach event, from literary festivals to campus orientations (parent orientation is particularly successful—many parents sign up both themselves and their incoming student!).
- A link to subscribe is included in library staff e-mail signatures.

- A checkbox with an option to subscribe to *Happenings @ Hannon* is included in every program online RSVP form.
- An option for adding an e-mail address to the mailing list is at the bottom of every program feedback form; this also enters attendees into a drawing for a hundred-dollar Amazon gift card each semester.

As of the end of January 2015, *Happenings @ Hannon* had 3,574 subscribers—nearly four times the initial number—and it continues to grow.

Content, Content, Content

After the initial work of selecting a vendor and identifying and building the audience for *Happenings @ Hannon* was complete, the Hannon Library communication team turned their attention to developing the content for the e-newsletter. Strategizing and developing content was—and continues to be—the most labor-intensive aspect of publication. The title of the e-newsletter lets readers know what to expect within—"happenings" at the library. The primary goal of *Happenings @ Hannon* is to keep the LMU community informed of activities at the library and to build audiences for the dozens of programs and exhibitions hosted each semester; this comprises approximately two-thirds of the content in each newsletter. The remaining articles and features highlight collections, resources, staff, or other news. A typical issue includes the following elements:

- Header photograph that changes monthly
- Letter from the editor
- Calendar of events and highlighted programs
- Recaps or announcements
- Featured photo that highlights the user experience
- Featured resource
- Links to library social media accounts
- "Give Now" link to donate to the library

Libraries considering launching an e-newsletter should carefully consider their audience (as described above) in concert with what kind of content that specific audience would find most valuable. As the William H. Hannon Library communication team explores targeted e-mails for faculty and donors in the future, the content may be much different; it needs to reflect the unique concerns and needs of those particular users and their relationship to the library.

At the William H. Hannon Library, the outreach and communications librarian takes primary responsibility for *Happenings @ Hannon*, although everyone in the library is invited to recommend content for the e-newsletter through monthly calls for content. Brainstorming and collecting content ideas, writing, art directing, and producing each issue of *Happenings @ Hannon* takes up to two full workdays each month. Members of the library's communication team and the dean of the library provide review and revision assistance once the first e-mail draft is completed. The tone of the newsletter is professional yet accessible. Hyperlinks are included wherever appropriate—usually to take the reader to the RSVP page for a program, or to the library blog for a full-length article. Featured resources link directly to the library catalog or e-resource, and the photo of the month links out to the original source of the photograph (typically a user's Instagram account). And in alignment with social media content best practices, an image accompanies most articles.

As with most social media, visual images in e-newsletters are essential to create interest and attract attention. The first iteration of *Happenings @ Hannon*, designed with a template selected from Constant Contact's menu of templates and customized with LMU school colors, was certainly functional enough. But after two years of using the same template, librarians saw a need for something that had more space to include compelling visual imagery and better aligned with LMU's institutional brand standards. During the summer of 2012, the outreach and communications librarian worked with Constant Contact's design team to create a custom template for *Happenings @ Hannon*, which both vastly improved the visual appeal and provided a more flexible, modular design for the newsletter (see figure 7.1).

CLICK SEND . . . NOW WHAT?

Open Rates and Click-Throughs

On September 13, 2010, the outreach and communication librarian distributed the first issue of *Happenings @ Hannon* to a mailing list consisting of 1,102 members of the LMU community. Now that it was "out there," it was time to answer the question, "Now what?" In other words: assessment. The basic objective measures of impact for e-newsletters are the "open rate"—the percentage of recipients to whom an e-mail is sent that actually opened it (as long as either the images load in their e-mail or a tracked link is clicked, the open is recorded)—and the "click-through rate"—the percentage of people who opened the e-mail and clicked at least one link. The open rate is handy for estimating general interest in the newsletter, and the click-through rate helps determine which specific articles or links are of most interest in each e-mail. Constant Contact provides their users with annual data about the average open rates across different industries (see figure 7.2). They do not segment "libraries" as a specific industry, so the library communication team chose to benchmark the newsletter's performance against nonprofit educa-

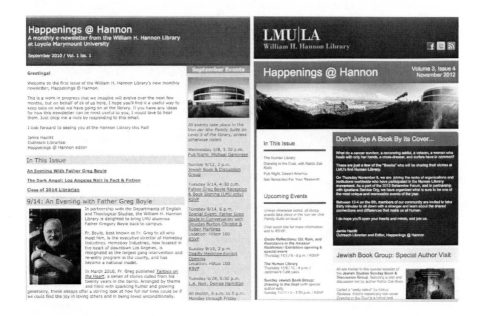

Figure 7.1.   2010 *Happenings @ Hannon* design alongside 2012 redesign.

tion and art galleries/museums, figuring that if it received an open rate between 20 and 25 percent, *Happenings @ Hannon* was on the right track.

The first newsletter had a surprising open rate of 36.5 percent and a click-
through rate of 25.2 percent, which surpassed both industry averages and the
library's expectations. The novelty of that first issue wore off slightly
though; for the next two academic years, the open rate ranged between 26
percent and 30 percent, and the click-through rate was as low as 5 percent for
some issues and as high as 25 percent for others.

Other vendor-provided measures that help assess the community's reception of the newsletter are tracking the number of users who choose to unsub-
scribe after receiving a specific issue, and users who mark your e-mail as
spam. Because the library communication team took care to build the e-
newsletter's audience by explicitly asking individuals to opt in, the unsub-
scribe and spam-report numbers for each issue of *Happenings @ Hannon* are
incredibly low; the library has not yet received more than two reports of
spam after sending any one e-mail, and maintains an average of only three
"unsubscribes" per issue.

Since the 2012 redesign, the open rate for *Happenings @ Hannon* has
held steady above 30 percent. And as the number of subscribers has grown
over the past five years, so has the open rate; the open rate for the January/
February 2015 issue was 35 percent. For the past three years in a row,

	Open rate	Click-through rate
Art Galleries / Museums	24.19%	6.45%
Non-profit (Education)	23.81%	7.67%
Happenings @ Hannon	35.40%	10.50%

Figure 7.2.   Open and click-through rate averages for nonprofit education, galleries/museums, and *Happenings @ Hannon* (Constant Contact, 2014a).

Happenings @ Hannon has been the recipient of an "All-Star" designation from Constant Contact, which recognizes excellence in reaching users through using best practices in e-mail marketing. Only 10 percent of the five hundred thousand small businesses and organizations that use Constant Contact receive this distinction (Constant Contact, 2014b), and the William H. Hannon Library is proud to have *Happenings @ Hannon* recognized in this manner.

Internal Assessment Measures

Internal assessment of the impact of *Happenings @ Hannon* has been more informal and subjective than the statistical measures provided by Constant Contact. As mentioned above, the primary goal of the newsletter is to communicate information about and build audiences for programs and exhibitions, so the library communication team felt it critical to develop a mechanism for assessing whether or not *Happenings @ Hannon* was meeting this goal. They attempted to capture this information by integrating the question "How did you hear about this program?" into all of the online RSVP forms for library programs. According to the data collected from these RSVP forms since 2013, *Happenings @ Hannon* has been second only to word of mouth (professor, friend, etc.) when it comes to drawing attendees to library programs (see figure 7.3). Print media and social media continue to be important parts of the Hannon Library's publicity strategy for library programming, but these results also validate the investment in *Happenings @ Hannon* as a core method for communicating about library programming. These results also inspire the library communication team to consider the potential impact and value of future e-newsletters to strategically communicate with more targeted audiences, such as faculty and library donors.

Anecdotal feedback about *Happenings @ Hannon* has also been overwhelmingly positive. Librarians are regularly approached by staff from other departments across campus who are interested in launching an e-newsletter for their unit and consider *Happenings* a model that they would like to follow. Shortly after the first issue was published, the library received acco-

"How Did You Hear About This Event?"
(data collected at library programs
September 2013 - February 2015)

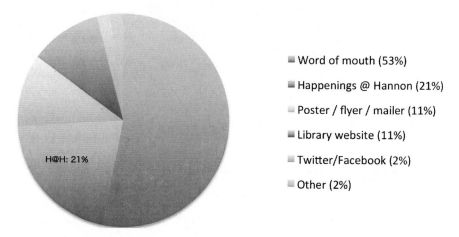

- Word of mouth (53%)
- Happenings @ Hannon (21%)
- Poster / flyer / mailer (11%)
- Library website (11%)
- Twitter/Facebook (2%)
- Other (2%)

Figure 7.3. "How Did You Hear About This Event?" statistics, September 2013 to February 2015.

lades from the president of Santa Clara University (a former dean at LMU), who was greatly impressed with the e-newsletter. And during a university presidential search committee listening session in October 2014, the subject of campus communication arose as an issue that a new university president must be concerned with; a faculty attendee highlighted the library as one of the few units at LMU who was "doing it right." Collectively, all of the information gathered since 2010 corroborates and affirms *Happenings @ Hannon* as an incredibly valuable tool in the communication arsenal for the William H. Hannon Library and for its e-newsletter subscribers.

WHAT'S NEXT FOR *HAPPENINGS @ HANNON*?

Happenings @ Hannon undoubtedly serves as an effective outreach tool for the William H. Hannon Library, but even the most successful initiatives can still be evaluated, improved, or expanded. The majority of library programming is open to all, and as such, the library's subscriber base for *Happenings @ Hannon* is deliberately very broad. As mentioned above, one of the next steps in our e-newsletter strategy will be to develop a dedicated e-mail outreach campaign for faculty and donors. Constant Contact—like many direct e-mail marketing vendors—charges a subscription fee based on the total number of subscribers, not the number of different messages sent. So it is possible to expand communication efforts to include newsletters for more specific audiences using the existing tools for which the library is already paying.

Moving forward, librarians will also pay more attention to the click-through statistics that Constant Contact tracks at the article level and use this information to evaluate the types of content that most resonate with readers. Librarians will determine which articles or events get the most click-throughs, and why, and how this information can be used to create even more relevant content for future issues of *Happenings @ Hannon*. The library communication team will improve adherence to e-mail marketing best practices, including the use of descriptive subject lines, creating more compelling headlines, and using even less copy in e-newsletter articles. The team will also develop strategies to increase the subscriber base using online tools, since current reliance on print sign-up sheets increases the likelihood of errors in transcribing handwritten subscriber e-mail addresses, which can result in bounced messages.

FINAL THOUGHTS

In the literature review in his article evaluating faculty preferences for e-newsletter format, librarian Alex Watson observes, "literature on the subject of newsletters [in libraries] is . . . very scant. Articles about online library newsletters tend to focus on the procedural, detailing how to build a newsletter, rather than the analytical, examining newsletters and readership after they have been established" (2011: 201). While the analysis conducted by the library communication team to date validates *Happenings @ Hannon* as a successful publicity tool, Hannon librarians agree with Watson that more can be done to discover what its readers find specifically useful about the e-newsletter, and what they might suggest to even further improve its value.

The communication landscape continues to rapidly change as social media tools come and go, and at the William H. Hannon Library librarians will continue to explore the utility of multiple tools in their efforts to make sure the library remains visible and effectively communicates its value to users. Over the past five years, *Happenings @ Hannon* has undoubtedly been one of the most successful and consistent means of reaching LMU users to promote programming and library news. The librarians at the William H. Hannon Library hope that the success found with *Happenings @ Hannon* at LMU might inspire other libraries to explore e-newsletters as a tool to improve communication and outreach with their communities.

REFERENCES

Aufreiter, Nora, Julien Boudet, and Vivian Weng. 2014. "Why Marketers Should Keep Sending You Emails." McKinsey & Company Insights & Publications, January. http://www.mckinsey.com/insights/marketing_sales/why_marketers_should_keep_sending_you_emails.

Constant Contact. 2014a. "The Average Open, Click-Through, and Bounce Rates of Other Constant Contact Customers by Industry." *Constant Contact Knowledge Base.* http://support2.constantcontact.com/articles/FAQ/2499.

———. 2014b. "What Is the Constant Contact All Star Award?" *Constant Contact Knowledge Base.* http://support2.constantcontact.com/articles/FAQ/2817.

Watson, Alex. 2011. "Library Newsletters in Print and Digital Formats: Faculty Preferences in a Hybrid Format." *Internet Reference Services Quarterly* 16, no. 4 (December): 199–210.

Chapter Eight

Increasing Library Use

It's a Long Story

Erica Thorsen — Albemarle High School Library

You may ask, "How did Albemarle High School Library market and promote itself, resulting in triple the usage and circulation in one semester?" It's a long story. Fairly recently, school libraries and librarianship have changed dramatically. The use of technology has revolutionized many aspects of the library—among them are the way librarians consider learning spaces, how they communicate with the school community, and the type of collection and resources they can offer our school community. In Albemarle County, librarians have made many changes in school libraries to move the vision from a traditional library to a post-Gutenberg learning and resource space. Embracing the four Cs—communication, collaboration, critical thinking, and creativity—and throwing in a few Cs of our own—choice and comfort—the library at Albemarle High School (AHS) has moved well beyond being just a book repository. Through creative publicity, promotions, and projects, AHS Library is now a place that strives to better meet the needs of its twenty-first-century learners, providing access to a wide variety of resources, ranging from technology and databases, to makerspaces and 3D printing, to a music studio (see figure 8.1) for the student response to changes.

BACKGROUND

Albemarle High School is the largest of three high schools located in Albemarle County, Virginia, with almost two thousand students and over two hundred faculty and staff members. Located in the urban center of the county, AHS is home to a diverse student population. Almost 8 percent of

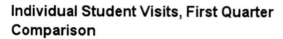

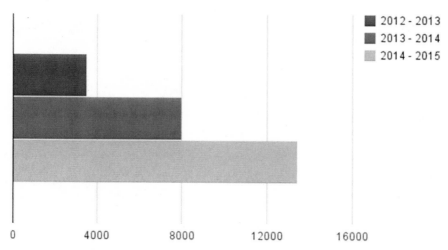

Figure 8.1.   Student response to library changes.

students speak one or more of over forty languages and, therefore, are enrolled in English for Speakers of Other Language (ESOL) courses. Just over 23 percent of the students receive free or reduced-price lunch. Eleven percent of students qualify for special education services. AHS boasts an active and enthusiastic student body with many academic and social clubs, honor societies, fine and performing arts, and athletics.

Libraries are in a time of exciting transition, and AHS was about to embark on a transition of its own! In the spring of 2013, both of the librarians who served the AHS community planned to retire. To lead this change, an elementary school librarian was transferred from a school within the same school division. Along with a social studies teacher turned librarian, the pair began to explore the library and imagine its bright future. The AHS principal saw a need for change and gave the new librarian team the directive that there needed to be a visible difference on day one of the next school year. The principal wanted the AHS community to know that they were walking into a different space. It was time to roll up our sleeves and get to work! The librarians' mission was to create a new renovated space—and widely promote and publicize it—so that the entire school community not only felt welcomed but also wanted.

When the summer began, the AHS Library was traditional in every way: structure, furniture, paper-book-centered collection—frankly, it was rather boring. The summer allowed the new librarian team the opportunity to spend quality time in the library and extensively review its collections, policies, and layout, while also studying best practices and new trends within school libraries. The new librarians spent many hours in the library going through everything—desks, files, folders, computerized records, and more (silverfish abound!). It was clear that the library needed a complete makeover. The added challenge was reimagining what the facility could become without losing the best-loved parts.

As seen in figure 8.2, there was copious signage that displayed in "thou shalt not" fashion what could not be done in the AHS Library. These rules that shouted an endless series of *do nots* were in direct contradiction to our principal goal: to make the library a warm and inviting place. The library should be a place to belong—to sit, stand, relax, study, research, read, communicate, collaborate, and create. It should convey a message of trust, collaboration, and community, not provide dated and obsolete policies and procedures. The new librarian team needed to develop policies and procedures that would encourage all of the goals (and things not yet thought of!) so as to communicate to the school community that the library had changed and the welcome mat was out. Oh, come ye all!

Based on ideas, research, and conversations with school and county leadership, the new AHS Library team developed the following goals, as well as provided ideas and recommended best practices for others interested in promoting and publicizing their own library:

- Taking spaces used for library offices and storage and returning them to students
- Updating the collection
- Capitalizing on Web presence and social media

CHANGING THE FOCUS: RETURNING SPACES TO STUDENTS

To accomplish the goals of creating a student-centered learning commons and seriously publicizing and promoting the library services, the physical space and layout of the library would have to change. Four of the rooms within the library housed librarians' offices and storage for VHS tapes and periodicals. There was a voluminous reference section in the middle of the library and an enormous circulation desk that dominated one of the walls of the library. Another section was devoted to a group of sixteen desktop computers arranged like a computer lab. There was a need for more variety in the types of learning spaces to meet a diverse group of learners. Since the AHS Library is a space where many different meetings, presentations, and classes occur, an arrangement focusing on flexibility and easy movement of furniture was paramount.

Figure 8.2.   You are welcome?

First Impressions Count: Lobby and Circulation Desk

Building a community based on trust and communication required some changes that the AHS community would notice as they walked in the front doors of the library. First, the security gates were removed in the hope that students would understand the subtle cue that the contents of the library belong to the entire school community—they would be trusted with those books and resources. The twenty-two-foot circulation desk also took up prime library real estate and was a visual obstacle to both students and staff. The librarians were able to get a much smaller circulation desk being discarded from a middle school in the same school division and relocate it to an area that was more obvious, apparent, and welcoming. Through a combination of building- and division-level funds, comfortable chairs and a sofa were added to provided seating for this area, giving us space for about twenty more students.

Making Room for Patrons: Reference Room Emerges and Offices Turned into Student Spaces

Examining catalog records, the librarians found that the majority of VHS tapes were not only never used but also contained outdated content. The periodicals sat largely unused as well, especially since many are available through electronic means. Huffing and puffing throughout August, the librarians successfully removed both the VHS cassettes and the periodicals. When the freestanding shelving was removed, it left a large space for student use. Simultaneously, the reference collection was evaluated; it was both dated and not heavily used, judging from the dust and cracking of the spine covers when opened. Outdated reference books were removed, and appropriate books were transferred to the circulating collection. The remainder of the reference books were relocated into a room dubbed the "Reference Room." The addition of area rugs, lamps, and a mix of comfortable seating and café-style tables made this a perfect room for quiet study. The furniture and accessories for this room consisted mostly of donations from the community, coupled with a few inexpensive purchases. This past summer, the crumbling tile floors were replaced with a faux wood laminate, and overhead lighting was replaced with dimmable LED lighting. As seen in figure 8.3, students find a haven for quiet work tucked away in our new Reference Room.

Three additional offices and storage rooms have also been reimagined and redesigned as student spaces. A room equipped with a table, chairs, and useful supplies (e.g., markers, crayons, different types of paper, scissors, glue sticks, and window markers) is now available for small groups of students to collaborate on school projects. It is also a popular space for tutoring throughout the school day and after school. Chalkboard paint was recently added to the main wall in that room, providing a collaborative and teaching component. The chalk wall has been a popular addition with tutors and students. A combination of math problems, social studies charts, and doodles dominate the wall.

Before   **After**

Figure 8.3. If you make room for students, they will come!

Another former office houses the College and Career Center. A specialized counselor uses the center as her home base, and students are welcome to work there throughout the school day. The center is now equipped with tables, chairs, and computers for small-group or independent research and work. A pleasant surprise that stemmed from moving the College and Career Center into the AHS Library has been that many of the visits from college recruiters also occur within the library.

Additionally, what was once a cluttered storage room is now a peer-tutoring center. Tutors are available before school, during lunches, and after school to assist students. The room has been transformed from a storage room to a comfortable space for students to work collaboratively, with a variety of types of furniture. A teacher recently said, "It's not a library, it's a student center," and that is a sentiment we could not have been more pleased to hear!

Both the College and Career Center and the Peer Tutoring Center help students and faculty see the library as a multipurpose facility. They also help expand the perception of what happens in the library, drawing a lot of curiosity and interest in the wide variety of activities that occur. The librarians, college and career counselor, and peer-tutoring teacher reach out to promote and share opportunities and work happening through a variety of channels such as e-mail, AHS newsletters to faculty and parents, the school website, and Twitter. Publishing images and examples is an effective way to publicize and promote while giving potential users concrete ideas.

Expanding Our Impact: Music Studio

As a division, Albemarle County Public Schools is moving toward a one-to-one laptop environment, thus eliminating the need for stand-alone computer labs. This past summer, a lab attached to the library was turned into a music lab. A cinderblock wall was torn down and replaced with a glass wall with the intention of allowing supervision and contagious enthusiasm for the experimentation with and creation of music. Many wonderful projects have been incubated in this music makerspace, including the following:

- Creation and performance of songs to meet the need of curricular projects
- Development of voice readings for read-aloud exams
- Exploration of software and relation to math concepts

Although the inclusion of the Music Studio as a part of the library may not seem like a natural pairing, it has served the AHS community well and provided excellent publicity for the library as a trendy learning and resource space. The diversity of students who regularly visit the library has blossomed as many students who did not step foot in the library last year are becoming avid users. Teachers appreciate how it has expanded library services that assist their students and the nuts and bolts of their work. The Music Studio has allowed the librarians to reach out to the school community in ways we never thought possible.

During division-wide professional development days, teachers and students involved in the Music Studio have also reached out to other division schools and are working with young students in a variety of ways. Students have taken some equipment to the elementary schools to show students how to use it. Through this outreach and connections with fine arts and music teachers throughout the county, elementary students have also sent beats and sounds for AHS students to use in their musical endeavors, once again promoting the library in a unique manner.

UPDATING THE COLLECTION

In June 2013, the AHS Library had a large print collection with an average age of 1989. The vast majority of the books were unused and in need of updating. An analysis of the collection found that nonfiction was largely unused. The circulation system was four years old, and many of the books had not been checked out at all in those four years. Sadly, looking at the information provided by vendors, it was apparent that the databases were underused. Throughout the year, extensive weeding and updating of the sections that saw usage was an important focus for the librarians. Currently, the average age of the collection is 2000—not perfect but much better. Removal of these outdated resources has also allowed us to remove several book-shelves, which opened up floor space for students.

Moving forward, nonfiction materials that will support curricular projects or that are specifically requested are purchased. When teachers develop a project or assignment and print resources are not available, the librarians order those resources and always follow up with teachers for future planning. This has proven to be an effective method for increasing collaboration with teachers and ensuring the nonfiction section is useful to the AHS community.

A large portion of the fiction section is based on student requests. To add visual cues and contribute to user friendliness, the librarians added genre labels on our fiction books. On the library website, a brief Google Form allows the librarians to easily take requests from the entire AHS community (http://bit.ly/1DpNOha). This type of economy with print book orders has allowed exploration into e-books. The reference works and e-books available through the Gale databases are fantastic for informational needs. To address the need for fiction and popular reading e-books, twelve Kindles are avail-able. The Kindles are "genrefied," and each has approximately ten heavily requested titles within each genre. It is simple to quickly add a title based on requests as well. Students have enjoyed the quick and easy access to several novels with one checkout. To promote the library and the use of its Kindles, the librarians have cataloged them so the titles are easily accessible to pa-trons. Also helpful, especially for browsing users, are physical reminders such as "dummy" books on the shelves where the book would be.

One of the librarians and an ESOL 3 teacher developed a culminating project to allow students to boost awareness of their home countries and cultures. This project, to be used as the students' midterm exam grade, incor-porated research, writing, speaking, communicating, and creating. As various types of art, time periods, and movements throughout history were presented and taught, students took notes in an art journal. ESOL 3 students reviewed that journal and selected one or more pieces of art they found inspiring and expanded to consider how that piece of art could be influenced by their home country or culture. Using materials, such as cardboard, fabric, beads, buttons, Styrofoam, paints, paper plates, and canvas, students constructed a piece of art. Students wrote about their inspiration and the intent and meaning of their artwork and then recorded their piece in the music studio. We developed a self-guided installation in the library in which the students' artwork was coupled with uploaded recordings. The recordings were linked with QR codes to make them easily accessible.

As a culmination for this project and to further market the AHS Library's updated collections, the librarians hosted a festive gallery opening. Invita-tions were sent to AHS administration, division-level administration, as well as students and faculty the students thought important. Students shared their work and explained the process to attendees. Then the artwork was displayed for the following month, which allowed the school community to see the project and outcome (see figure 8.4). The school's broadcast class captured various stages of this project on film and pieced together footage and shared the video on AHS's morning announcements and also with other schools and divisions. The AHS Library and cultures of the ESOL students were truly highlighted in this student-made product.

Cold War Museum Project

Not all change comes easily, and the evolution of the AHS Library certainly had its share of growing pains. Notably, some of the teachers were hesitant to embrace a student-centered space. Cognizant of that, the AHS librarian team partnered with two history teachers who were open to using the specialized library resources and spaces. The students were about to begin their study of the cold war and the civil rights era, and the teachers wanted the students to get a true feel of the turmoil and unrest of the time period. Along with an instructional coach, the librarians developed a museum and combined resources—real and virtual—to expose students to the time period. A collection of *Life* magazines and yearbooks from the era were displayed alongside laptops full of images, songs, speeches, and videos on tables. Having divided the time period up into four subtopics of the Civil Rights Movement, Cold War Foreign Policy, Cold War Significant Events, and Life at Home during the Cold War, students could take their time visiting each station. Students immersed themselves in many primary sources and rich audiovisual resources over the course of several days. To ensure that students experienced and understood the main concepts, they completed a Google Form to share what they learned with their teachers. Partnering with adventurous and instructionally tolerant teachers was beneficial in having the faculty as a whole see that the changes in the library allow more effective collaboration and use of library resources for instruction. For more on the museum, see https://sites.google.com/a/k12albemarle.org/cold-war-era/.

CHANGES IN SPACE LEAD TO A SHIFT IN PRACTICE

In what might be the corollary of form follows function to the space, the configuration of the library led to changes in practice. AHS librarians needed to figure out ways to better meet the needs of modern learners. Starting out, these are a few things that stood out as important to students:

Erica Thorsen

Figure 8.4.   AHS community comes together in library.

- 24/7 access to resources
- Desire to understand the "why"
- A diverse collection of tools

To meet the needs of our 24/7 mobile learners, a redesigned website was imperative to give students increased access to the library and its resources. The redesign created a more user-friendly and intuitive website and served as a major promotional tool for the "new" library. Often, when teachers begin a research project with students, a Web guide customized for that project and posted on the website is helpful. In the Web guides, specific databases and resources that will be most helpful for the project at hand are highlighted. Also provided are screencasts with instructions so students can revisit them at any time. Students can complete their research anytime or anywhere with a librarian's guidance.

When a class visited the old library, the databases how-to was the main area of instruction. On the plus side, it is helpful for students to understand the features of supportive research databases. However, moving toward a one-to-one laptop and continuously connected environment, there is a need for many different types of instruction. Along with research skills, the importance of information literacy and digital citizenship is a necessary component of instruction. Librarians developed a module on the AHS Digital Learning page of the Albemarle High School Digital Learning Site (https://sites.google.com/a/k12albemarle.org/ahs-digital-learning-site/students)   to assist with awareness and instruction in the following areas: safety and security, digital citizenship and responsibility (digital footprint), cyberbullying, and intellectual property and citations. The module was presented to staff and students on "Tech Tuesday," a digital learning day that occurred early in the school year. Participation in Tech Tuesday and assisting in this way has helped the librarian team be seen as instructional partners and resources for teachers wishing to develop further related instruction.

Expanding Services with Makerspaces

As makerspaces are playing a larger role in public and school libraries across the country, the library team thought it would help facilitate more creative interactions and a greater sense of belonging to the AHS Library if they expanded and marketed services in this way, providing timely, accessible, and inexpensive ways to have those experiences available for the AHS community. There are many supplies to help students complete projects—markers, crayons, paper, rulers, glue sticks, and so on, but we really wanted to delve into making a variety of different types of things. A couple of fun making opportunities that have required a small amount of time and financial investment have been Make Your Own Bookmarks (using either origami paper or paint-chip samples or special markers) with Community Based Instruction Program students, and BYOP—Bring Your Own Pen and embellish it with ribbon and fabric.

On the more technical side of making, a Silhouette Cameo, two Arduino kits, and a MakerBot 3D printer have been obtained. Using the Arduino kits, students are experimenting with circuitry and programming. The librarians aim to develop a "Coding Cave," which will be the home of the Arduinos and similar tools that are on our wish list, such as the Raspberry Pi (http://www.raspberrypi.org). Tables are also being purchased.

The Silhouette Cameo has gotten a lot of use from teachers and students alike. Teachers are fans of its ease of use and flexibility for bulletin boards and displays. Students have enjoyed creating larger displays such as posters for projects and signs for elections and school events.

The 3D printer has attracted a lot of attention from students creating for both class and personal interests. At first, students were amazed when they would download and print items from Thingiverse (http://www.thingiverse.com), but they quickly moved on to designing original items. Several classes including Computer Aided Design and World History I have incorporated 3D printing into projects.

Publicizing Maker Opportunities: World History I 3D Project

An AHS social studies teacher was anxious to use the 3D printer as a component of his class. Together, the teacher and librarians developed a project in which groups of students selected and researched Ancient Roman artifacts using library books and databases. Students then reverse engineered their selected artifact and replicated it on the Maker-Bot. Since third-grade students also study Ancient Rome, it presented a natural opportunity to connect via Skype with third-grade classes in two elementary schools in our school division. The World History I students taught the third graders about their artifact, its historical significance, and the process of replicating this artifact on the 3D printer. This innovative and enjoyable project allowed for the publicizing of makerspace opportunities within our school and in the greater Albemarle County area. AHS teachers saw ways to incorporate 3D printing and making into seemingly unlikely subjects areas. One of the Albemarle elementary schools involved in the Skype visits was awarded a grant to obtain their own MakerBot and are now creating 3D products for students and staff there. Additionally, Charlottesville, Virginia, is now host to an annual festival of innovation and entrepreneurship called the TomTom Festival (http://tomtomfest.com/events/geniushour/). The librarian team and social studies teacher brought equipment and artifacts from this project to share at the Genius Hour portion of the festival, garnering interest from many community members.

SPACE UTILIZATION, COLLECTION UPDATE, AND PROGRAM PRACTICE: BEST PRACTICES

Throughout the reenvisioning and updating process of the library, the AHS librarian team researched, questioned, polled, and strove to provide the most effective spaces and programs for the school community. Having put ideas into action, the following are best practices as seen by the library team at AHS.

Returning Spaces to Students

- When creating student spaces, look for bar-height tables, circular tables of a variety of styles and heights, and comfortable chairs and sofas that offer students a lot of comfort and choice.
- To meet the needs of a wide variety of patrons and tasks, reimage spaces currently used for storage and adult offices.
- To encourage student-centered use of the library, keep posted rules to a minimum.
- Embrace the opportunity to widen the reach of the library by housing nontraditional services. For example, the College and Career Center, Peer-Tutoring Center, and Music Studio at AHS Library.

Updating the Collection

- To ensure that patrons can easily locate specific types of fiction books, add genre labels.
- To easily accept requests from patrons, use a brief Google Form, e.g., AHS Library's Book Requests Google Form (http://bit.ly/1DpNOha).
- To address the need for fiction and popular reading e-books, purchase some e-readers and then "genrefy" them (i.e., add about ten heavily requested titles within each genre). AHS Library purchased twelve Kindles, and it was simple to quickly add a title based on requests. Students have enjoyed the quick and easy access to several novels with one checkout.
- To increase communication and collaboration with teachers, follow up when resources are received for specific projects or assignments.
- For promotion of virtual materials, such as e-books, the suggestion is to have physical reminders in the library.

Changes in Space Lead to a Shift in Practice

- Use information and resources included on the EGUSD Digital Citizenship Resources for 21st Century Teaching and Learning website (http://blogs.egusd.net/digitalcitizenship/about/).
- For better accessibility and to help students adapt resources to best meet their learning styles, have library laptops preloaded with excellent free resources, such as Balabolka (text-to-speech software, http://download.cnet.com/Balabolka/3000-2170_4-75182534.html), Clearly (makes websites easy to read, http://download.cnet.com/Evernote-Clearly/3000-11745_4-75805658.html), or Speak It! (text-to-speech software, http://download.cnet.com/Speak-it-Text-to-Speech/3000-2124_4-10974046.html).
- To encourage buy-in from the school community, reach out to adventurous and instructionally tolerant teachers and collaboratively develop and teach effective lessons.
- To move toward digital curriculum, have the library play a major part in the development and implementation of information literacy and digital citizenship instruction.
- To develop a makerspace, start with a variety of items and invest more heavily in those that patrons gravitate toward.

CONCLUSION

Though often misquoted, the sentiment in the adage "If you build it, they will come" rings true in regard to the AHS Library. With less than six hundred dollars, a change was sparked. Throughout the changes, we were pleased by student responses. Our students come to the library in droves and are our largest supporters. The AHS Library team capitalized on word of mouth, social media, and partnerships with adventurous teachers to promote our student-centered space. The team continues to look to the needs of our students and explore ways the Albemarle High School Library can evolve to best meet those needs. We are looking forward to seeing what the future holds!

Chapter Nine

If You Build It, Will They Come?

Marketing a New Library Space

Coleen Meyers-Martin and
Lynn D. Lampert—Oviatt Library,
California State University, Northridge

BACKGROUND

The California State University, Northridge (CSUN), Oviatt Library successfully completed an eight-month, multifaceted communications and marketing campaign that promoted a two-and-a-half-million-dollar renovation of a new Learning Commons. This chapter articulates how the project's promotional goals and objectives tie into furthering the Oviatt Library's mission of serving more than thirty-eight thousand students. Specific tools and actions used to carry out the promotion and the rationale for their inclusion within the programming are addressed. Details such as staffing, funding, and the time involved to coordinate a two-phase marketing campaign provide insight into the many logistical details needed to manage a grand-scale project. User community reaction due to the promotion and the assessment tools and techniques utilized within the campaign are included as well. Best project management practices, including our implementation action plan, are shared with the hope of helping others embarking on a promotional campaign to promote a new library space or renovation.

DESCRIPTION OF THE CAMPUS, THE LIBRARY, AND THE LEARNING COMMONS MARKETING PROJECT

In 2012, CSUN's Oviatt Library began developing a major marketing campaign to inform the campus community about its plans to renovate existing library spaces to open a dynamic Learning Commons space with new supporting services. To carry out this Learning Commons project, the library partnered with several campus divisions, including the campus Information Technology (IT) division, Student Services, and the University Corporation. The shared efforts to incorporate an IT help desk staffed with IT workers and student assistants, build a new full-service coffeehouse for all visitors within the library, and relocate CSUN's Learning Resource Center with math and writing tutoring services within the library required considerable planning and collaborative strategizing. In light of all of these new services and the anticipated construction impacts that would occur in several busy areas within the library itself, the marketing campaign needed to accomplish many things for several different target audiences, including students, faculty, staff, community users, and potential external supporters.

CSUN is the second-largest California State University campus in a twenty-three-campus system and serves more than thirty-eight thousand students in the San Fernando Valley of Los Angeles. As a Hispanic-serving institution, CSUN's student body is made up of 38 percent Latino/a students, and 44 percent of the overall campus population originates from traditionally underserved ethnic communities. CSUN's Oviatt Library is located in the center of the 356-acre campus and serves as the main library with a collection of more than 1.4 million physical volumes. The library's collection also boasts approximately 600,000 e-books and more than 150 academic-based databases. Among the library's primary goals are to support classroom and independent learning and to facilitate student and faculty research. The library is heavily frequented with 4.8 million uses of its Web pages annually. Approximately 1.4 million people visit the library, and a team of twenty-eight librarians field approximately twenty-seven thousand reference questions virtually and in-person each year. As a teaching institution, the Oviatt Library provides approximately twenty-four thousand students with library instruction sessions annually. During these sessions, librarians guide students on how to find and evaluate credible and scholarly information for university-level research papers. The Oviatt Library has a dedicated outreach program that serves and reaches many non-CSUN and CSUN communities. For the last ten years, a dedicated tenure-track librarian has served as the coordinator of outreach services alongside other librarians who serve on the outreach committee.

While the Oviatt Library continues to be a popular and highly visited location on campus, its last significant building renovation, prior to the

Learning Commons project, occurred following the 1994 Northridge earthquake. The 6.7-magnitude earthquake severely damaged the integrity of the library's structure, and the aftermath of the disaster required years of reconstruction and repair before students and faculty could once again utilize the library's physical space. However, more than a decade had passed since the earthquake renovation project had completed its course.

Many major campus and library stakeholders had been discussing, for some time, the possibility of providing the library with a significant physical upgrade. Ultimately, campus stakeholders supported a two-and-a-half-million-dollar renovation project to develop a library Learning Commons that would foster the development of the twenty-first-century student and scholar. Their vision called for creating a multifunctional and flexible space that could further integrate the library into the lives of students. After many months of planning, coordination, and construction, the Oviatt Library now boasts a Learning Commons that integrates the new skillsets of librarians with twenty-first-century technologies; provides students with ergonomic, portable, and flexible furniture; provides a light and open space; is food friendly; and facilitates a teaching and learning dynamic. The new Learning Resource Center facility is now housed on the third floor of the Oviatt Library, allowing students to comfortably receive tutoring services within the library, where they may choose to remain and study individually or within a group.

CHIEF OBJECTIVES AND CARRYING OUT OUR MARKETING CAMPAIGN

Planning for this groundbreaking renovation project and the new Learning Commons offerings drove the library to develop a comprehensive campus communications and marketing campaign. This formal marketing campaign assisted library stakeholders in communicating the importance and details of the physical construction project to the campus community while simultaneously informing all campus and community members about the many new resources and services that would be available within the library's new Learning Commons. The goals of the campaign were (1) to inform students, staff, faculty, and the community about the construction project and what the new Learning Commons would provide, and (2) to build anticipation and excitement for the upcoming Learning Commons resources and services and grand opening event. Library stakeholders and librarians also identified this marketing need as an opportunity to confer with campus marketing experts in order to develop a marketing plan that would meet users in as many formats and mediums as possible. Developing a communications campaign to encompass these goals required strategy and planning with a myriad of communication vehicles that were carefully paced over the course of eight months. The strategy included phases due to the university's semester calendar and schedule.

Assessing the need for a carefully paced and multifaceted promotional campaign included consideration of the many dynamics involved in disseminating information to a diverse community on such a large campus. Prior to the start of the renovation, interactions with students and campus faculty during library lectures, at the reference desk, and at campus committee meetings revealed that many within the campus community were not aware of the future renovation and library Learning Commons offerings. To help bridge communication and the sharing of information, librarians and staff coordinated interactive in-person sessions with CSUN students in which they were given the opportunity to "design" a library Learning Commons they would like to see and utilize on their campus. Students created diagrams of potential library Learning Commons physical spaces that included desired features, such as more group study rooms and lounge areas. These student drawings were assessed by the architects and project management team to help develop the design and layout of the Learning Commons. As an initial first step within the marketing communication process, these sessions also served to inform students of the forthcoming construction project, enable assessment of student needs, and apprise library stakeholders of student desires and expectations. This experience also exposed students to the opportunity of what a Learning Commons could provide and how it may potentially impact their learning processes while at the library.

Another initial step taken to develop the Learning Commons marketing campaign involved assessing library users and demographic information. Library administration considered their core user groups, including students, staff, faculty, and community members, and they considered what these user groups wanted in an academic library (New Mexico State Library, 2014). The use of surveys, comment cards, and suggestion boxes are some common vehicles to determine this type of information. Other ways of gathering this information include informal brainstorming sessions with staff members, the use of focus groups, mining census data, and talking directly to users (Alman, 2007). Library administrators found that students, in particular, wanted more group study spaces, moveable and ergonomic furniture, technology, and more support for utilizing that technology. Once demographic and user information had been gathered and assessed, it was included within the development of the Learning Commons marketing plan. Following the assessment of user groups, library administration moved forward and created an in-house marketing team specifically for the campaign, as the library does not have a marketing department or dedicated marketing staff member.

Launching a marketing campaign for a major renovation and the unveiling of a new space can be both intimidating and exhilarating all at the same time. While the Oviatt Library had carried out promotional campaigns prior to developing this marketing plan to help launch the Learning Commons, staff had not embarked on such a large marketing project. This undertaking presented numerous known challenges heading into the project, including a compressed timeline, a finite budget, and limited internal marketing expertise. Our marketing campaign had to encompass a twofold mission of (1) informing students, staff, faculty, and the community about the construction from both a safety and user-awareness standpoint as we remained open for operations during all construction, and (2) building awareness and excitement for the upcoming Learning Commons resources and services and grand opening event in the fall of 2013. In addition to these pressures, library leadership and staff also knew that they needed to communicate with faculty and students about both the anticipated print collection relocations and necessary weeding from the Reference Room collection to make room for the new dynamic study spaces that the Learning Commons would occupy. As Metz and Gray cautioned in their article "Public Relations and Library Weeding," advance notice and strong and clear communication about physical changes to any collection help ward against poor public relations and negativity toward new library programming (Metz and Gray, 2005).

Those selected to serve on the marketing team included librarians and staff members whose regular responsibilities and roles within the library deemed their participation essential for a communications campaign. More details about the specific members within the team and their roles within the project will be discussed later in this chapter. Once established, the newly designated library marketing team invited a campus marketing professor to assist in the development of a comprehensive campaign. The marketing professor collaborated with the team by creating and providing a communications campaign that would be implemented within a strategic timeline. The marketing plan included goals and objectives as well as strategies for carrying out the plan (Alman, 2007). Several members of the marketing team worked with the library dean to customize the plan to align with the library's allocated budget and resources for its implementation. Evaluation methods for the effectiveness of the campaign were also considered at this stage in the process.

A catchy tagline for the campaign—"Share the Commons Experience"—was developed, and specific communication and marketing strategies were designed to be carried out in two phases. The library does not have an official logo as mandated by university protocol. Therefore, the "Share the Commons Experience" campaign tagline design served as the logo for the project (see figure 9.1). "Share the Commons Experience" was included on all of the campaign's promotional materials and served to brand the project and message. Special consideration was given to the academic calendar since most students and faculty would be leaving in mid-May for summer break and

Figure 9.1. "Share the Commons Experience" logo.

would return in early August for the fall semester. This required the campaign messages to be timed accordingly. Both phases of the campaign included tactics that focused on raising awareness of the library renovation and created anticipation and excitement about the new Learning Commons and its offerings. Both social media and traditional media platforms were targeted for distributing messages. During the spring of 2013, Phase 1 of the campaign aimed at creating a buzz about the construction project and about the many offerings the new Learning Commons would provide. Phase 1 of the communications task also included communicating service changes and collection relocation information to all library visitors. Once students returned to campus after summer break and in early fall, Phase 2 continued to promote the upcoming Learning Commons offerings and build excitement for the grand opening event.

VEHICLES AND STRATEGIES FOR COMMUNICATING THE MARKETING MESSAGE

Selecting varied marketing and communication vehicles is an important step in message design within any promotional effort (Mathews, 2009). The multifaceted marketing campaign was devised and structured to reach library users in the medium and format they most frequented. An online campaign reached those users through Facebook, Twitter, Instagram, YouTube, and the library's website. The library website banner promoted information about the upcoming Learning Commons construction project and future Learning Commons offerings. A library blog also reported on the project in addition to several pages on the website that were dedicated to providing answers to questions about the construction project and future Learning Commons. The library marketing team also orchestrated an online giveaway of a Samsung tablet. Due to a generous donation from one of the library's database vendors, Sage Publications, librarians and staff developed a Facebook contest in which students who "shared" about the Learning Commons on Facebook would be entered in a drawing to win the tablet.

Several videos were developed throughout the eight-month promotional period and were released during different phases of the project. An initial introductory video (http://tinyurl.com/kpfmllo) was created and released on the library's YouTube channel and sent out by e-mail in late spring to reach faculty and students before the summer break. The video informed the campus community about the renovation project and provided details about what the new Learning Commons offerings promised. In spring, several time-lapse cameras were put into place within the Learning Commons construction areas in order to capture the renovation process. This footage was later used in a time-lapse video that showed library users firsthand the construction efforts that had taken place to develop the Learning Commons. The time-lapse video of the construction was edited by a cinema and television student, posted to the library's YouTube channel, and sent by e-mail to many on campus (http://tinyurl.com/kfurdnc). Midway through the promotional campaign, a librarian, two staff members, and a cinema and television student filmed and edited a "Learning Commons" video (http://tinyurl.com/mfdgoqo). Several minutes in length, the video describes the planning and construction processes as well as the promises of the Learning Commons. The video includes interviews with the campus president and other major stakeholders and was released on the library website and YouTube channel and sent by e-mail during the fall semester as another online vehicle to promote the new Learning Commons offerings.

More traditional elements of the promotional campaign included the distribution and posting of banners, lawn signs, posters, A-frame posters, and flyers that were developed by several librarians and the library's in-house graphic artist. These materials were distributed throughout the dorms and campus grounds at the beginning of the spring and fall semesters. Student assistants helped with the distribution of these materials. Several outreach booths provided library passersby with information about the Learning Commons and its offerings and a chance to win free movie passes. Inside the library, users were greeted with colorful banners in the lobby and in the future Learning Commons area. These banners provided descriptions and images of what the Learning Commons promised for the campus community. To create further interest and enthusiasm for the project and new Learning Commons, library staff wore "Share the Commons Experience" T-shirts and buttons on assigned days so that everyone using the library on that particular day was greeted with the tagline. Campus newspaper ads communicated the message of the upcoming Commons. These ads were interactive in that they provided students with an opportunity to complete a puzzle within the ad to win a free "Share the Commons Experience" T-shirt. Messages were artfully chalked on campus sidewalks to inform those as they walked from class to class and to parking lots. Finally, table tents at campus eating locations and coffee sleeves on the campus Freudian Sip coffee cups also communicated the details about the Learning Commons and grand opening event.

Throughout the eight-month campaign, library marketing team members collaborated with campus colleagues in the planning of the grand opening event that would celebrate the new space and offerings. The community at large was informed of the new Learning Commons offerings through press releases that were sent to local press outlets publicizing the event and welcoming campus and community members. Two hundred and eighty-five people attended the grand opening event, including students, campus faculty, staff, and community members who enjoyed hors d'oeuvres and listened to a live jazz band and grand opening speeches. Library marketing team members collaborated with campus music faculty to arrange for the musicians. The team also coordinated with the campus IT division and facilities departments for sound and ground management services. The campus food services collaborated with the library to provide food and rentals. Reaction to the grand opening event and the launch of the Learning Commons was overwhelmingly positive.

HOW THE PROMOTION FURTHERS THE LIBRARY'S MISSION, USER COMMUNITY REACTION, AND INITIAL ASSESSMENT

Since the Learning Commons opened in the fall semester of 2013, the first floor of the Oviatt Library has become the most popular spot for students to study and work collaboratively on campus. While the new coffeehouse, located in the library's lobby, has drawn many students into the building, undoubtedly the new comfortable and spacious seating, along with the addition of new technologies and well-appointed group study rooms, has kept the students in the building actively collaborating and studying during all open hours. The new look and feel of the Learning Commons has helped foster renewed awareness of the Oviatt Library's mission and services. By drawing more individuals into the library, the addition of the Learning Commons has introduced both students and faculty to existing library services throughout the building. This helps the library promote its mission to support the diverse information needs of its academic community through the delivery of relevant library resources and services through partnerships with CSUN faculty and staff in the education of our students (Oviatt Library, 2012). In addition, the new Learning Commons also helped the Oviatt Library strive further toward its vision statement, which envisions "providing a dynamic and comfortable space for study and teaching that is conducive to different types of learning styles, including quiet study and collaborative interactions" (Oviatt Library, 2012). With the Learning Common's marketing campaign promoting awareness about new and existing services, both prior to and after the grand opening, all visitors were more apt to make use of services, such as making online advance group study room reservations, using course reserves services, and seeking assistance from reference and instructional programming.

The *Sundial*, the CSUN campus student newspaper, ran many stories about the Learning Commons project during the marketing campaign, which helped raise student awareness. The reaction of the students, as reported in both written stories and video-recorded student interview segments (http://sundial.csun.edu/2013/09/new-oviatt-library-learning-commons-is-a-big-hit/), was very positive and reflected that the project was both well understood and received (Scrabano, 2013).

When assessing the overall success of the promotional campaign, it is clear that the time, budget, and effort invested in the in-house library marketing strategies ultimately paid off with the positive campus reception to the new Learning Commons. Group study room reservations increased by 28 percent within the first year of Learning Commons usage. It is also telling that all of the Learning Commons partners contributed financially to the final success of all adopted marketing platforms. From the promotional coffee cup sleeves supported by the University Corporation to the popular microfiber screen cleaners that celebrated the collaborative nature of the project across campus divisions, every facet of the promotional campaign was shared and discussed. Because of this, the marketing team decided to allocate a reasonable amount of the overall budget toward giveaways and contests aimed at increasing student interests.

Student participation within social media promotions, all contests, and Learning Commons launch events outlined in the appendix to this chapter was high in relation to previous promotions. Reservations to attend the grand opening event were closed one week early due to an overwhelming response. Attendance at the grand opening event reached full capacity (figure 9.2). Through the use of campus press releases and strategic placement of marketing tools in both print and digital formats, news of the grand opening event and new Learning Commons even reached nearby local media outlets, such as the Santa Clarita public television station, which hosted an online story about the event (Santa Clarita Public Television, 2013).

STAFFING, FUNDING, AND TIMING CONSIDERATIONS

One of the first steps that had been taken by library administrators, staff members, and librarians involved in the promotional campaign was to create an in-house library marketing team. The team included several librarians and staff members, the library dean and associate dean, the library webmaster and webmaster assistant, an in-house graphic artist and videographer, a communications staff member, a Learning Commons assistant, campus marketing faculty who served as consultants, and many library student assistants. One librarian served as the lead for the promotional campaign in communicating and coordinating the marketing plan that had been created by the faculty member who served as the marketing consultant.

Meetings were held every few weeks in an effort to discuss the details and logistics of implementing the multilayered campaign. Frequent meetings enabled those on the project to address unanticipated issues that arose and provided lead time to adapt various elements of the programming when necessary. Most often, members on the team volunteered for various aspects of the promotional project that related to their regular work assignments. Team members created time for the promotional project within their existing work schedules. Sometimes it was necessary for team members to temporarily set aside other programming and projects within their regular work areas

Figure 9.2.   Grand opening event. Courtesy of Lee Choo.

in an effort to develop the promotional print and online materials, including several videos. The marketing team also coordinated the grand opening event, which ultimately served as a culmination of the promotional and marketing campaign. A key facet to the overall success of our marketing plan grew out of the implementation action plan that the marketing team adopted and developed with the assistance of the campus marketing expert (see appendix to this chapter). All promotional devices and details were outlined in this plan and timeline right down to the date that the outdoor sidewalk chalking activities would be launched to promote the new Learning Commons.

Historically, the Oviatt Library's budget for promotion and marketing has been nominal. However, due to the significance of the renovation project and the anticipated impact on the campus community, the library dean's office approved additional funding for a print promotional campaign, online giveaways, and the grand opening event. The library utilized the "objective-and-task method" in order to determine the amount of funding to invest in the marketing programming (Fisher and Pride, 2006). Within the objective-and-task method, the library determined its budget by defining its marketing objectives and tactics and the estimated costs of implementing those measures. The sum of the costs was the proposed marketing budget for the campaign. When the costs reached a level higher than the amount of funding the dean had approved, the team revisited their proposed tactics and strategies and pared down the costs when and where necessary.

The Oviatt Library has a special fund that is associated with donors for such programming. Other ways of acquiring and securing funding and donations for marketing purposes include the following:

- Collaborating with campus and community partners to provide services and resources for the programming
- Requesting donations from vendors, in particular database vendors
- Receiving financial donations from campus and community members
- Utilizing special library-donated funds and grants

MARKETING STEPS FOR THE FUTURE

The promotion and marketing of the library renovation and new Learning Commons offerings during the spring, summer, and fall of 2013 marked the initial marketing efforts on behalf of the library's marketing team. However, the Learning Commons has continued to expand its services and resources since the grand opening event and promotional campaign that concluded in the fall of 2013. Initial marketing efforts are currently under way to promote the addition of a new Learning Commons Creative Media Studio (CMS) that is newly available to CSUN students. Through the use of social media, physical tours, campus online and print publications, and in-library signage, students are discovering how the CMS is a designated space to create multimedia projects with iMac workstations. Marketing efforts highlight the equipment and software available to students, such as Pro Tools, Final Cut Pro, and Photoshop. There is also mention of student assistants within the CMS who are on hand to provide support with utilizing the technology. The marketing team has also included the promotion of a soundproof recording studio, video and audio recording devices, headphones, a scanner, and more. Through its initial marketing efforts utilizing social media promotion, physical in-library signage, and campus publications, the library marketing team is promoting the new CMS within the Learning Commons as a comfortable, technological, and social space.

BEST PRACTICES FOR COORDINATING LIBRARY MARKETING CAMPAIGNS

Marketing library resources and services may commonly involve large projects, such as promoting a new Learning Commons, but just as often they will involve more specific communications programming, such as in the promotion of a single new service or resource. The following are suggestions and recommendations for coordinating and managing promotional efforts no matter the size of the marketing and communications campaign.

Get organized. Create a marketing plan for your project. If you do not have a marketing staff member within your library for these purposes, look to see if your institution already has existing resources or a person within your organization who could serve as a marketing consultant. You may even want to consider hiring a consultant. Supplement your promotional efforts with books that specifically discuss library marketing and programming. Many books are available that outline and describe the library marketing plan processes. Utilizing them to structure a marketing campaign to fit your library's specific size and marketing needs can make the development of a plan less daunting. Overall, many library marketing plans will typically be varied in length and content according to their institution's size and goals. Marketing plans with smaller goals may only be several pages long, while more ambitious marketing campaigns may require a plan several times that length.

When developing your marketing plan, keep in mind that most plans include the following: library demographic information, a SWOT analysis (strengths, weaknesses, opportunities, and threats), marketing project objectives and goals, a marketing strategy and tactics to be utilized to carry out the strategy, a list of team members who will carry out the plan, project costs and funding information, and methods for evaluating the promotional campaign

(Alman, 2007). Other issues to consider when developing a marketing plan include the following:

- Create a timeline and schedule for your marketing plan. Distribute the plan to all team members.
- Hold regular meetings to discuss programming and implementation needs.
- Ensure someone is specifically assigned to each task; if no one is personally assigned, realize that no one will be accountable.
- Scan your environment to see if there is talent or interest in the project by staff members, even if they are not in your area. See if it is possible to invite them to participate.
- Collaborate with campus and community partners. These types of collaborations can produce additional assets, such as funding, donated items, and the time and assistance of additional personnel. Such partners can also communicate the message of the campaign within their professional circles.
- Look at other award-winning library marketing campaigns for ideas and inspiration. The John Cotton Dana Award winners' website (http://john cottondana.nonprofitcms.org) provides a list of many successful marketing campaigns, big and small.
- Plan accordingly, but be open to changing the plan if necessary.

CONCLUSION

Today's libraries must rely heavily on marketing and promotion to remind users of the unique benefits that their services and collections offer. Whether a library is undertaking a new project, planning for a major renovation, or promoting new or existing products, programming, or services, it is imperative that marketing messages are well received by the target audiences the organization serves. Unfortunately, librarians do not traditionally receive formal training about marketing practices in graduate school. However, with proper planning and collaborative partners, in-house marketing strategies can succeed when creatively coupled with knowledge of your library clientele's demographics and needs. Key factors needed for success include assembling a dedicated team to work on marketing needs and diligently working to ensure that each promotional facet will be delivered within the planned timeline targets and budget. The Oviatt Library's marketing team succeeded in completing its multifaceted communications and marketing campaign to promote a two-and-a-half-million-dollar renovation of a new Learning Commons by developing a feasible and creative marketing action plan that maximized the benefits of both traditional media and social media communication platforms.

REFERENCES

Alman, Susan Webreck. 2007. *Crash Course in Marketing for Libraries.* Westport, CT: Libraries Unlimited.

Fisher, Patricia H., and Marseille M. Pride. 2006. *Blueprint for Your Library Marketing Plan: A Guide to Help You Survive and Thrive.* Chicago: American Library Association.

Mathews, Brian. 2009. *Marketing Today's Academic Library: A Bold New Approach to Communicating with Students.* Chicago: American Library Association.

Metz, Paul, and Caryl Gray. 2005. "Public Relations and Library Weeding." *Journal of Academic Librarianship* 31, no. 3: 273–79.

New Mexico State Library. 2014. "Library Marketing Plan Workbook." http://www.nmstatelibrary.org/docs/development/planning/Marketing_Plan_Workbook.pdf.

Oviatt Library. 2012. "Mission, Vision and Values." http://library.csun.edu/About/Mission.

Santa Clarita Public Television. 2013. "CSUN to Dedicate New Learning Commons." *SCVTV Blog,* September 24. http://scvtv.blogspot.com/2013/09/csun-library-to-dedicate-new-learning.html.

Scrabano, Ken. 2013. "New Oviatt Library Learning Commons Is a Big Hit." *Sundial* Video Archive, September 9. http://sundial.csun.edu/2013/09/new-oviatt-library-learning-commons-is-a-big-hit/.

APPENDIX: MARKETING ACTION PLAN, OVIATT LIBRARY, LEARNING COMMONS, CALIFORNIA STATE UNIVERSITY, NORTHRIDGE
SHARE THE COMMONS EXPERIENCE!—FALL 2013

Raising Awareness: February to May 2013

- Stakeholder presentations to select group of students, faculty, and staff (carried out by library dean, associate dean, and department chairs)
- Classroom presentations (carried out by librarians)
- Department presentations (carried out by library administration and librarians)
- Public relations—campus newspaper: meeting with editor, construction tour, constant updates; media alert 8/13: grand opening press release (carried out by associate dean and library communications staff member)

Implementation

Phase 1: Building Anticipation "The Learning Commons Is Coming"

 4/16/13—Launch the Learning Commons Marketing Campaign: The goal of Phase 1 is to create buzz that the Learning Commons is coming. The date or details will not be revealed at this stage.

 4/16/13—Online Marketing: Begin posting "Share the Commons Experience" on Facebook and #campaigntagline on Twitter. Run ads on the library website banner. Create library Web page and blog describing the Learning Commons construction process and upcoming offerings of the new Commons. All online marketing tactics will have a link to the library website. (Carried out by two librarians, webmaster, and webmaster assistant.)

4/16/13—Chalking: Chalk "Share the Commons Experience" and library.csun.edu/evolution by Sierra Tower and Freudian Sip, University Student Union. (Carried out by student assistants overseen by librarian or staff member.)

4/16/13— Lobby Signage: Hang one large banner in the lobby that reads "Share the Commons Experience" and has the blog URL, in addition to two column banners that advertise the Commons. Two Learning Commons "safety" posters (due to construction) will be placed within the entrance of the lobby (entrance and exit of escalators). These posters will describe the construction timeline. Five adhesive window messages that say "Pardon our dust during construction" will be placed on entrance doors. (Carried out by in-house graphic designer, librarian, and staff member.)

4/16/13—E-mail Message: Send an e-mail blast message to library subscribed members and all campus communicators with "Share the Commons Experience" and a link to the Learning Commons blog. Ten lucky winners who reply "I'm in!" will receive a Learning Commons giveaway. Instructions will be prominent on the oviatt.csun.edu home page. (Carried out by library communications staff member and librarian.)

4/16/13—Sundial Ads: Run print and online/mobile ads beginning 4/16. These ads will inform readers of the upcoming Learning Commons. Several of the ads will include contests such as completing a crossword puzzle, Sudoku, and matching games in order to win a "Share the Commons Experience" T-shirt. (Carried out by in-house graphic designer and librarian.)

4/16/13—"Share the Commons Experience" Printed Materials: 155 posters, 5,000 fliers, 20 lawn signs, 20 A-frames, and 3 banners (1 Eucalyptus and 2 USU). All printed materials will include a QR code and the URL for the blog. The QR code will link to a video after May 6. (Carried out by in-house graphic designer and librarian.)

4/16/13—"Share the Commons Experience" Buttons: Provide all library staff and student assistants with promotional buttons. Everyone in the library will wear buttons to entice questions regarding the grand opening. When asked about the button, participants will give out a "Share the Commons Experience" flier. (Carried out by in-house graphic designer, librarian and staff member, and student assistants.)

5/1/13—400 "Learning Commons" Internal T-Shirts: Staff and student assistants will be given "Share the Learning Commons Experience" T-shirts to wear and promote the Commons. (Carried out by student assistants managed by staff member and librarian.)

5/1/13—Freudian Sip Coffee Sleeves: "Share the Commons Experience" coffee sleeves will be distributed to all Freudian Sip locations on campus. Twelve cases of coffee sleeves, which equates to 14,400 sleeves made with Recycled Newspaper. Main goal is to raise awareness about the Learning Commons. (Carried out by in-house graphic designer and librarian.)

5/6/13 —The "Learning Commons" Video: Introduce the "Learning Commons" video on the library's website, YouTube, Pinterest, Facebook, and Twitter. (Carried out by an in-house video production team that includes two staff members, librarian, and student assistant. A library communications staff member helped to distribute the video once it was completed.)

5/6 to 7/31/13—Continuation of Phase 1: Lawn signs, posters, banners, and flyers displayed within the library and on campus grounds. Online marketing also continued with the use of social media.

Phase 2: Grand Opening Ramp-Up

8/1/13—Introduce Phase 2 of the Learning Evolution Campaign: This phase will focus on the promotion of the grand opening. The grand opening date will be introduced. Marketing materials must include the date or a countdown timer.

8/1 to 8/24/13—New Student Orientation: Set up promotional booths at each day of orientation to provide giveaways and promote grand opening. Present information via video and in-person presentations. Five thousand grand opening fliers distributed at NSO booths as well as at the library, dorms, Redwood Hall, Sierra Hall, USU, SRC, SSU, and targeted classrooms throughout campus. (Volunteers to serve at the booths [approximately ten] and materials will be coordinated by a librarian. The volunteers can be librarians or staff members.)

8/1/13 to October Opening—Online Marketing: Post "Share the Commons Experience at the Grand Opening on October 3" on Facebook and #LearnCommons on Twitter. Introduce countdown timer on the front page of the Oviatt website. Send an e-mail blast message to your listserve. Run ads on the Oviatt website banner. (Carried out by two librarians, library communications staff member, and webmaster.)

8/1/13—"Share the Commons Experience" Printed Materials: 155 posters, 2,500 fliers, 20 lawn signs, 20 A-frames, and 3 banners (1 Eucalyptus, 1 on library, and 1 at USU). All printed materials will include a QR code and the Oviatt/Evolution website. (Carried out by in-house graphic designer, librarian, staff member, and a team of student assistants.)

8/1/13— *Sundial* **Ads:** Run print and online/mobile ads beginning 8/1. These ads will promote the grand opening and include a contest to win a free "Share the Commons Experience" T-shirt. (Carried out by in-house graphic designer, librarian, and staff member.)

8/1/13—Chalking: Chalk "The Commons Experience Is Here!" along with grand opening details, the event date, and website by Sierra Tower and by Freudian Sip, USU. (Carried out by student assistants overseen by staff member or librarian.)

8/24/13—Table Tents: Table tents promoting the Commons and the grand opening will be placed on tables in the Plaza del Sol, OST Lawn, and all TUC food courts (Library, Arbor Grill, Freudian Sip, Sierra Center, Geronimo's, Pub Sports Grill, and Book Store Food Court). (Carried out by in-house graphic designer, a librarian, and several student assistants.)

8/24/13—Dorm Displays: Print approximately seventy twenty-two-by-thirty-four posters with grand opening graphics to place on each floor of campus dorm displays. (Carried out by in-house graphic designer and team of student assistants managed by a librarian.)

8/24/13—Start of Facebook Contest: Have library's website banner promote "Share the Commons Experience" and link students to a set of instructions. For example, "Share the Commons Experience on Facebook." Enter those that share about the Learning Commons grand opening in a raffle to win a Samsung mini tablet. Place posters and fliers on each floor of the library to promote the Facebook contest. The winner will be announced soon after the grand opening and featured on the library's blog. (Carried out by two staff members and a librarian.)

9/13/13—Marketing Tables: On three separate occasions, set up marketing tables with fliers and giveaways to promote awareness about Learning Commons. Give away popcorn, candy, and T-shirts and offer students an opportunity to enter in a raffle for two movie passes. (Volunteers of several librarians and staff members coordinated by librarian.)

9/13/13—Time Lapse Learning Commons Video: Introduce the time lapse "Learning Commons" video on the library's website, YouTube, Pinterest, Facebook, and Twitter. (Carried out by an in-house video production team that includes two staff members, librarian, and student assistant. A library communications staff member helped to distribute the video once it was completed.)

Day of Event and Mid-October

10/3/13—Online Marketing: The goal is to create buzz about the grand opening. Start posting comments like "The Commons Experience Is HERE!" on Facebook and #learningevolved on Twitter. Send an e-mail blast message to the library listserve, and run ads on the website. Add event to campus calendar of events and submit a request to the CSUN webmaster to have the event on the CSUN home page. All online marketing tactics will have a link to the Oviatt blog URL. (Carried out by two librarians, webmaster, and library communications staff member.)

10/3/13—Ten Grand Opening Two-by-Three-Foot A-Frame Posters: A-frames will be strategically placed by Sierra Quad, Sierra Food Court, Redwood Hall, Chaparral Walkway, Fitness Centre, Arbor Grill, Matador Bookstore, and the Oviatt Library. Work with AS, USU, MIC—borrow additional A-frames. (Carried out by staff member or librarian and a team of student assistants.)

10/3/13—Twenty Grand Opening Lawn Signs: Grand opening lawn signs will be strategically placed on the east and west sides of the Oviatt Library. (Carried out by staff member or librarian and a team of student assistants.)

10/3/13—Grand Opening Banner: Hang one large grand opening banner in front of the library. (Carried out by staff member and librarian.)

10/3/13— *Sundial* Ads: Run half-page *Sundial* ads for three consecutive days beginning on the day of the event announcing the opening and offerings. (Carried out by in-house graphic artist and librarian.)

10/3/13—Grand Opening Giveaway: Distribute 285 special Learning Commons–branded microfiber cloth giveaways at the event. (Carried out by in-house graphic artist, librarian, and team of student assistants.)

10/14/13—Introduce the "Making of the Learning Commons" video on the library's website, YouTube, Pinterest, Facebook, and Twitter. (Carried out by an in-house video production team that includes two staff members, librarian, and student assistant. A library communications staff member helped to distribute the video once it was completed.)

"Implementation Action Plan" based on marketing plan by Kevin Lizarraga.

Chapter Ten

Marketing on a Shoestring

Publicity and Promotion in a Small Public Library

Heather Nicholson—Coaldale Public Library

I got my start in marketing in one of my very first jobs. At the age of twenty, I was hired by my university's international center to help to publicize international student exchanges to my fellow students. Among other things, it involved making promotional announcements at the start of the semester in all classes containing more than three hundred students. I was painfully shy and it was terrifying, but it worked. My boss was a trailblazer in terms of on-campus guerilla marketing, and his department was hugely successful. It was largely under his mentorship that I began to appreciate that it doesn't matter how terrific your product or service is if no one knows about it, and you cannot rely solely on word of mouth to spread the message.

I have never aspired to work on Madison Avenue, and yet in almost every paid and volunteer role I've taken on since that job, marketing has been an essential element of success. Now, in any given week as the head librarian of the public library in Coaldale, a community of about 7,500 located in Alberta, Canada, I can be found running a book club, ordering new library materials, weeding the collection, updating a policy manual, attending a community meeting, repairing a leaky toilet, setting up for a videoconference, or ordering office supplies. But if you ask me what the most important part of my job is, I will tell you that it boils down to marketing.

The concept of marketing is relatively new in the work environment of librarians. Not long ago, marketing was considered a "dirty word" by information professionals, who associated it with slick sales techniques aimed at getting consumers to buy products they did not need. Some librarians still believe that as a public good, libraries should not have to be promoted or peddled to the public. John Buschman (2005) is a notable proponent of the argument that the benefits of libraries and many other public institutions cannot be easily measured or quantified, and as such should not be subject to economic-based business models.

Is there inherent good in preserving the knowledge of our civilization through the storage of books? Absolutely. Is access to information a core element of democratic discourse? You bet. Is it realistic to think that public libraries can maintain high rates of usership and compete for limited public funding by resting on the laurels of being a public good? Not a chance.

Fortunately, librarians' aversion to marketing and publicity is changing. There is a wealth of books, blogs, and newsletters dedicated specifically to library marketing, and marketing courses are regularly taught as part of library and information science programs. The shift began in the early 1970s when, largely due to the influence of Philip Kotler, people outside of the business sector began to understand the true nature of marketing and how it could be usefully applied in nonprofit organizations such as libraries (Kotler and Levy, 1969). Marketing is, in fact, a management tool that enables an organization to communicate with stakeholders, remain relevant, and provide high-quality programs and services. Marketing a library is practically synonymous with managing a library. It boils down to a two-way conversation to find out what your community wants and needs and to communicate to them what you can and are doing to meet those needs.

If you're lucky enough to work for a large urban library system, you may have the advantage of a marketing department staffed with professionals trained in the communication arts. If you're reading this, maybe you do not have such luxuries and, like it is for me, marketing is just part of your very long job description. Fortunately, librarianship is a community built on sharing, and many of the ideas I use are borrowed and adapted from others. Without the advantages of a large budget or dedicated professionally trained communications staff, it is possible to conduct effective marketing. Every community is unique and you have to figure out what will work for you, but there are some general strategies I have gleaned and share in this chapter from my experiences that can be applied to almost any small library.

IF YOU BUILD IT . . . : THE IMPORTANCE OF STRATEGIC PLANNING

Just because the cake pan lending library, genealogy club, makerspace, or writer's circle was a roaring success in Anytown Public Library, doesn't mean it's a good idea in your library. I read about interesting and innovative library ideas every week. My inner enthusiastic kid wants to try them all. In fact, one of the advantages of a small library is that there is a lot less bureaucracy standing in the way of me and my next big idea. Last year, while visiting a larger urban library, I noticed they had pulled all of their parenting books from their nonfiction collection and placed them in a dedicated area in their children's area. It seemed like a brilliant way to make that material more visible and accessible to parents who usually come to the library with small children. The Coaldale Library had the space to implement this idea, and after getting input from my staff, we made it happen the very next week. Patrons have offered a lot of positive feedback, and circulation of those items has been brisk. So how do you know what's going to work? Sometimes a little trial and error is in order, but before investing time in planning and marketing a program or service, figuring out what your community wants and needs is time well spent.

In the province of Alberta, where the Coaldale Library is located, in order to receive government grants, we are required to develop a "plan of service" outlining goals and objectives at least every five years. We are encouraged and most of us do use the model outlined by Sandra Nelson (2008) in Strategic Planning for Results. What is good about this process is that it gets to the heart of community needs and not just library users' desires. For example, in the last strategic planning process, we heard loudly from community members that our town was lacking in a central source of information about community events, activities, and services. As a bedroom community of a larger urban center, most Coaldale residents leave the town each day for work, and most of the information they get from the radio, newspaper, and social media is about events in the city. Helping remedy this challenge wasn't an obvious role for the library, but it became one of the library's key strategic goals over the last few years. While the problem isn't entirely resolved, some significant steps forward have been taken. Previously, the library had a small community bulletin board that was cluttered with community notices. Realizing how many people used this board as an information exchange, a board almost three times the size was installed. Talk about an easy and low-cost solution! In addition, we used the library's relationship with other community agencies, including the municipality, to advocate for the establishment of a monitored online community calendar of events. While the library doesn't host or maintain the calendar, it is used to promote library events and drive readership to the calendar through marketing efforts on social media and in newsletters. Library staff also increased efforts to work with other community service agencies to cross-promote events and services. Spending time and money on community awareness initiatives is addressing a community need. Similarly, when any other new idea presents itself, it's wise to refer back to the library's strategic plan and consider whether that initiative will help to meet the needs of the community before proceeding.

Simply put, you can market the heck out of anything, and you might even get some people to buy into what you are selling. On the other hand, if you find an existing need to fill, marketing is simply a case of informing people of your solution and the "product" sells itself.

FIGURE OUT YOUR BRAND OR VISUAL IDENTITY

Imagine how hard it would be to find your favorite brands in the grocery store if every time you showed up they had a new label, logo, or type of packaging? As exciting as it can be to open up a new document on your desktop publisher and start playing around with fonts and colors and graphics, not only is that extremely time consuming, but it is a terrible idea. Just because libraries don't have the budgets of multimillion-dollar companies doesn't mean there aren't things we can learn from what they do. One thing corporations do very well is branding. With their distinct logos and taglines, and by tying their products to a certain image or emotion, they are instantly recognizable. Once a consumer knows they like a brand, they expect it to be consistent and will keep coming back. The general perception about public libraries is already quite positive; we can build on that positive sentiment but need to be easily recognizable. Once we have won over patrons with great products and services, they need to be able to recognize the library brand when they see it.

The Coaldale Library had a logo in use for many years, but over time it became very dated; it was not consistently used, and it did not communicate the message that the board and staff wanted to send about the role the library played in the community (see figure 10.1). Every person walking into library building was given a disapproving look by the stern owl. The owl held a book, which reinforced the commonly held public perception that libraries are all about books. While this is a central and historical part of what libraries do, emphasizing the library as a community hub is an important message about where we are going in the future.

As a symbol of wisdom, owls may be considered a rather cliché image for a library. However in this case, we decided to stick with the owl. One of the unique features of the Coaldale community is a birds of prey rescue and conservation center. Its presence in the community for over twenty years is a source of local pride, and using the image of a raptor makes sense for that reason. Furthermore, our municipality, which incidentally provides most of the library's funding, also uses a stylized bird's wing in its logo; keeping the owl theme helps to reinforce the community brand.

With the approval of the library board, I began to rebrand the library. This can be an expensive process, and professional designers are worth their billing rates. If funds are available for professional design help, it is a great idea and probably money well spent.

Figure 10.1. The old Coaldale Public Library logo.

But there are alternative routes. Some designers will do pro bono or discounted work for a nonprofit or public organization that they support, like a library. Sometimes all they want in return is an endorsement or reference. In our community, another nonprofit organization had a new logo designed in exchange for a reference by a young graphic designer looking to build her portfolio. She agreed to work on a few ideas for the library as well; however, a job opportunity took her to another city before developing a suitable design. Another option is to consider that many college and university marketing or design programs offer their students practicums or real-world, project-based assignments. We contacted an instructor in the Communication Arts program at a nearby community college. Every year, students complete a capstone project working with a real client (usually a nonprofit). Initially, all we wanted was a new logo, but we were encouraged to expand the scope to give the students a broader experience. In the end, the students conducted a detailed market research survey of library patrons, a SWOT analysis. They redesigned the library logo (see figure 10.2); created a tagline; developed a style guide for the library's newsletter, brochure, and other print materials; created a series of print ads to promote the library's services; and provided us with a yearlong, low-cost advertising plan. All of this work was done for the library at no charge.

The new logo still uses an owl, but the new owl looks much friendlier and modern. The image of a book is also still present, but the inclusion of earbuds and the universal Wi-Fi symbol indicates the library's connection to the ever-changing digital world. The students also provided us with a second modified version of the logo (see figure 10.3) to be used when repetition is needed and the original logo has already been used. This alternate logo includes a tagline for the library: "The living room of the community."

Ever since being introduced to the idea of a "third place" as described by Ray Oldenburg (1989) in his influential book *The Great Good Place*, I have been intrigued by the idea of the library as "the living room of the community." Third places are described in community development literature as social surroundings separate from the two usual social environments of home (the first place) and work (the second place). Third places are very important for building civic engagement and establishing a sense of belonging. They are anchors of community life and facilitate and foster broader, more creative interaction. Some of the key characteristics that Oldenburg uses to describe third places include being free or inexpensive, highly accessible, and operating on regular hours. All of these are key qualities of a public library, and the library is an ideal candidate to serve as an important "third place" for Coaldale. I often used the expression "living room" when describing my vision for the library, and the students picked up on this as an ideal tagline. As such, we have not only a refreshed image for a brand but a tagline that communicates the story we want to tell about the library.

Working with students isn't as "turnkey" or simple as contracting the work to a seasoned professional. There are some downsides. First of all, the work needed to be completed on the college's schedule, which meant the opportunity was only available once a year during a short window. The students' deadline also happened to coincide with a very busy time of the year at the library, yet I had to make myself available to give the students feedback frequently with fast turnaround times. This was particularly challenging, since I wanted to involve the staff and library board as much as

Figure 10.2.   The new Coaldale Public Library logo.

Figure 10.3.   The new Coaldale Public Library logo with tagline.

possible in the process but had to limit their involvement somewhat to support the students' timeline. Second, given the students' inexperience and the fact that the library was not actually a paying client, there were limits on how many modifications could be requested. As a result, there were some marketing materials the students developed that we are unlikely to use. Overall, we were pleased with the result and appreciated the energy and passion the students showed for this project, but relying on volunteer or student work does come at a cost and it's important to be aware of this at the start.

Now that the library has a brand, we are working hard to apply it consistently. In the past, each time promotional materials were created for a program, we would use a different font, image, or color. With the new logo, we were given a style guide outlining the specific fonts and colors to be used on all of the library's promotional material. All that is needed is to enter basic information such as dates and times into existing templates and push that content out to the various print and online channels. Since I do most of the marketing work, this is not too difficult, but I do need to monitor myself and other staff to keep the message and image consistent.

We are also applying the principles of branding to each library program as well. For each program, one image has been selected (usually a high-quality photograph purchased from a stock image site or taken from clipart as appropriate) that will be consistently used to market that program, whether it is on the website, bookmarks, posters, or other places. In the past, for each new season of Small Wonders (our preschool storytime), a new poster was designed with different colors and images. It makes sense that once people are familiar with one image, it will begin to stand out for them when they see it in the future. While there is no way to be certain whether the consistency in marketing accounts for higher turnouts in the last year, it seems to be a contributing factor.

MARKETING DOES NOT HAVE TO BE EXPENSIVE

The Coaldale Library's annual marketing budget is four hundred dollars, and some years not all of this money is spent. Spending your marketing money and time judiciously and purposefully is far more important. Two years ago we put up a library billboard in a local hockey arena for the winter season. I did this because a provincial library body had funds available specifically for this purpose, and all I had to do was fill out a short application to be eligible. The billboard would have cost $1,500 had we purchased it ourselves. Given that Coaldale is in a wintery climate and hockey is a popular sport, it wasn't a terrible idea, but there is no evidence, anecdotal or empirical, that it made any impact. On the other hand, a foray into Facebook ads more than doubled the library's Facebook followers in one week and cost only forty dollars. That seems like great value for money.

Even the Coaldale Library's major rebranding initiative was not very expensive to implement. Printing new business cards, changing library signage, and printing T-shirts for staff and volunteers featuring the new logo cost less than one thousand dollars. We are fortunate to have an active and supportive "Friends of the Library" group, who agreed to incur many of these expenses. We've economized with stickers of the new logo to avoid reprinting business envelopes (we send so little paper mail anymore) and a few brochures. The advantage of so much communication being digital is that there is no reprinting cost for a website, electronic newsletter, or e-mail signature.

As part of the library's annual survey, patrons are asked how they find out about the library's offerings. The top two answers are our website and the monthly community newsletter that the town sends out with utility bills. Both of these marketing vehicles require some staff time, but they don't incur extra expense, and they work. A little staff time, an Internet connection, and a decent printer (preferably color) can make a big impact.

HOW DO YOU KNOW IF IT'S WORKING?

Another advantage large corporations have over public libraries is market research budgets. They can find out exactly who buys their products and target advertising dollars accordingly. Apart from anecdotal examples, it can be difficult to know if your marketing is successful or which efforts are the most effective. Once again, not having a huge budget doesn't mean this can't be done on a smaller scale. I really try to be open and encourage feedback from patrons by asking questions on social media or inviting comment through my monthly column in a local paper. There are also some more systematic techniques we use to evaluate the effectiveness of marketing efforts.

Every October we conduct an annual patron survey. This is part of the library's reporting requirements for the government. The government insists we ask about patron satisfaction with staff and services. This provides an opportunity to ask other questions to gather feedback about how people currently find out about library programs and events and how they would like to find out about them in the future. These survey results indicate that the website and newsletter are the most effective tools the Coaldale Library uses. Furthermore, when time is tight, that information helps to prioritize what marketing avenues need to be given the most attention and which ones are of less importance. For the annual survey and at almost every other major public event, a small enticement is offered in the form of a draw. Everybody likes free stuff, and many librarians have a stockpile of surplus, preprint, or donated books in great condition. Add a few chocolates, candles, or other treats, wrap it all up with a pretty bow, and voilà, you have people's attention. At special events, we encourage people to enter the draw and we ask on the entry form how they heard about the event. As an added bonus, posting a picture of the winner with their prize on social media makes for great public relations.

For programs that run regularly, asking participants how they heard about the program can be a great icebreaker and the first step toward building a relationship with them. The longest-running public program is the Wednesday morning early literacy program for preschoolers and caregivers. The staff member who has been running the program for the last twenty years is a master at this. She ensures everything for her program is set up well in advance. That way, as the caregivers begin to arrive with their children, she uses the time to learn the names of new faces and ask each one how they heard about the program. Later, she passes that information on to the rest of the staff to inform future practice.

STRETCH YOURSELF

When gathering evidence about the tools that work best, use every vehicle and platform available to communicate your message. When I first started in Coaldale, I took the time to make a list of every possible avenue to market the library (see figure 10.4). As you can see, the list includes free events, places to hang posters, and community e-mail lists. I update this list a few times a year, and over time, it has grown. Every time I want to publicize a library event or program, I have this checklist at the ready. Every avenue can't be used for every program or event, but the list helps ensure that nothing is forgotten and as wide a net is cast as possible.

It's important to always be on the lookout for new promotional ideas. For example, at the checkout desk, we give each patron a bookmark with the item due date stamped on it. Previously, a generic library bookmark had been made up for this, but occasionally the library would be provided with free bookmarks sponsored by a business or government agency wanting to promote themselves. It seemed crazy for the library to be advertising for someone else when we should be promoting our own events and services. Now, a new bookmark is designed for each month highlighting upcoming events or new services. A volunteer photocopies and cuts these up, so not a lot of staff time is invested. Now every person who signs out an item leaves with marketing material in their hands. My next project is to look at advertising in the library's public washrooms. Restroom billboards are so commonplace now that one may almost resent not having anything to read when in an empty stall. Because I normally use our staff bathroom, it wasn't until recently that I considered our public washrooms as an entirely untapped marketing opportunity, especially given the number of people who come into the library only to use the washroom. The intention is to market services that are perhaps underused or lesser known, such as some of the library's online databases. This will help give these services some exposure without requiring a lot of staff time to change up the material very often.

Event _____   Date(s) _____

	Select	Complete (date & initial)
Email		
Area school librarians		
Library board members		
Friends of the library		
Sunny South News (local weekly paper)		
Free events column		
Press release		
Lethbridge Herald (local daily paper)		
Community calendar		
Arts calendar		
Press release		
Town's monthly newsletter *(deadline is 20th of the previous month)*		
Chamber of Commerce		
Coaldale Community Connections interagency group		
Other:		
Posters/Displays		
Food market bulletin board		
Library		
Town office		
Chamber of Commerce main street board		
Community center marquee		
Sportsplex marquee		
Other main street businesses by request:		
Social Media/Online		
Coaldale community calendar online		
Twitter		
Facebook		
Library website		
Facebook community pages		
Other:		
Publications		
Library newsletter		
Due date bookmarks		
Community Learning Council brochure (published in September and January)		
Three-times-yearly town leisure guide		

Figure 10.4. Coaldale Library event publicity plan.

Sometimes stretching yourself means being willing to let others contribute their ideas and feedback. Some of the best sources of novel ideas are patrons and staff, especially newer ones. Many of the major changes implemented at the library were ideas that occurred to me within the first few months of working here. While I was cautious not to swoop in and shake things up too dramatically or suddenly without having a good understanding of this library, new eyes are fresh eyes, and they often see things that people who work in a place every day fail to notice—as evidenced by the patron who noted a punctuation error in a prominent sign that had been in place for several months in the library.

I ask every new staff member and many volunteers to complete a questionnaire within their first two weeks of working here. It asks detailed and thought-provoking questions about the way the library is laid out and designed, and the messages that are conveyed to them as they look around the library. While not every survey results in a dramatic overhaul of the library, it provides a new perspective and sometimes results in minor changes. For example, the library has several small, brightly colored tables that were previously used as patron workspaces. Occasionally, one or more of these tables were placed in front of the circulation desk for display purposes. New staff pointed out that these were, in fact, the most prominent and visible displays in the library. Given that the library doesn't have a shortage of other patron workspaces, these tables are now permanently located in this merchandising position. Displays and promotional materials for the library's most important upcoming events and programs are placed on these tables, and they continue to garner a lot of attention.

YOU *MUST* USE SOCIAL MEDIA

If your library does not have a social media presence yet, go and open a Facebook account immediately. While you're at it, you might as well get a Twitter account, too. The fact is your patrons *are* online. According to a 2013 article in the *Financial Post*, fourteen million Canadians check their Facebook newsfeed every single day (Oliveira, 2013). The Pew Research Center reports that 71 percent of adults are on Facebook, and while growth has slowed, user engagement with Facebook has increased (Duggan et al., 2015). Add to that number the people who use Twitter or Instagram or check Facebook once a week, and the statistics can make your head spin.

One example of how social media worked is the Coaldale Library adult book club. The book club started about two years ago after a patron suggested it on our Facebook page and a number of other Facebook followers agreed that it was a community need. Because social media allows users to engage with one another, an idea that may have been mentioned to us in person or by e-mail by one or two people, and possibly ignored, became a discussion and then a reality. The group meets monthly: it's well attended; several book club members have since become members of the Friends of the Library, and one has joined the Library Board; they are all active library advocates; and even people who can't fit book club meetings into their lives say they love our reading list, so it has turned into a form of readers' advisory, too!

One of the challenges of Facebook is that you can't guarantee all of your posts will be seen, but I have had some good results with Facebook ads. I like that Facebook allows you to specify who you want to target for an ad. Ads can be targeted by gender, age, or location, and it gives you feedback on the reach of the ad so you can get a sense of its impact. Earlier, I mentioned the ad campaign that targeted all Coaldale residents—it more than doubled the "likes" on the library's page in five days! As our base of followers increases, we get more "shares" and "likes" of our content, which in turn increases our base of followers. Combined with a few targeted ads now and then, social media is working for us. We haven't yet moved onto Pinterest and Instagram, but these are being considered.

Employing a social media management tool such as Hootsuite can help make managing your social media presence more convenient. Hootsuite allows you to monitor multiple social media networks at once and to schedule posts in advance, so if you don't have time to get online every day, your library page can be updated even when you are busy or away on vacation.

NETWORKING

One area where I still have a lot of room for improvement is to get out from behind my desk and talk to people. There will always be e-mails to respond to, reports to run, and spreadsheets to analyze, but spending time in touch with your community is essential in order to serve them well. Some might use the word "advocacy" to describe this work and not think of it as library marketing, but advocacy certainly falls under the larger umbrella of marketing. Some of the best feedback and ideas I get come from conversations with patrons at the circulation desk and community leaders I meet at public events. Apart from the marketing aspect, it's amazing what people will volunteer to do for you when you have conversations. From offers to write grant proposals to a community agency handing over a check, you never know when you might find yourself rendered speechless.

In a small community, word of mouth can be one of the fastest and most effective communication tools. To make it work for you, you've got to be out there repeating your key messages to as many people as possible. Make time to attend community service group meetings, talk to town councilors, get to know the school librarians, and build relationships. The payoff is invaluable.

In the last two years, I have been a part of getting an interagency committee up and running in Coaldale. It started out very informally with four members, including the library, the municipality, a nonprofit focused on adult learning and literacy, and a family social service agency. This group started meeting every six to eight weeks to share the different programs and initiatives we were working on and our perspectives about what gaps there were in meeting community needs. This was the venue we used to push for the establishment of an online community calendar, which is now operated by the municipality, and has led to other successful relationships and partnerships. We have written letters of support for one another's grant applications, cross-promoted events for one another in our newsletters and on our websites, and partnered on hosting some community events such as Family Literacy Day. Over time and through word of mouth, this committee has grown to include the local seniors' group, community outreach officers from the police force, school representatives, and more. Knowing more about the services and happenings in our community makes us better able to serve our patrons, but it also means more people are sharing our message.

An important aspect of this is knowing your strategic plan and having a few "elevator speeches" or short, targeted messages at the ready. Spend some time deciding on the most important things you want people to know about your library, or—to put it another way—the story you want to tell about yourself. Be prepared to work that into as many conversations as possible when you are networking with community leaders. During our last municipal elections, when the incumbent mayor was asked for his view on libraries, he referred to the library as "more than a structure that contains books, toys, computers and various forms of media, it is a place for the community to come together." I was thrilled to hear that the mayor (who was reelected, by the way) basically paraphrased the library's tagline before we even finished rebranding ourselves. This let me know we were doing something right; not only is the message getting through, but having other people repeat it has just multiplied our marketing efforts.

LOOKING TO THE FUTURE

I read marketing blogs and look to the community of my fellow libraries for new ideas. In the next year, there are two initiatives I want to pursue. One is to bring library awareness to the community by establishing more "Little Free Libraries" in the community. We have one at a rural community center, but establishing more could have several benefits. First, by placing them in busy community places, such as the hockey arena or children's playgrounds, they will be a visible reminder of the library to people who are not yet part of our patron base, especially if advertising about newer and online services is included. Second, giving people with time on their hands (i.e., waiting for their kids at hockey practice) a book to read will help build goodwill and remind people that libraries are all about sharing. And finally, it's potentially a great way to give a second life to materials withdrawn from the library collection.

Another initiative I'd like to pursue is the creation of a promotional video about Coaldale Library. If grant funding can be secured, I'd like to hire a student from the new media program at the nearby university to turn patron impact stories into a short but engaging video. Hopefully, this can be used for advocacy, marketing, and new patron recruitment.

CONCLUSION

What I love about working in a small public library is that I get to do a little bit of everything. Sometimes that is also the very thing that can be overwhelming. Fortunately, having a passion for library marketing makes it easy to continually want to grow and innovate. In some small communities, the library is one of the few public institutions thriving. What libraries do, often on shoestring budgets, is extraordinary. It's a story worth marketing.

REFERENCES

Buschman, John. 2005. "Libraries and the Decline of Public Purpose." *Public Library Quarterly* 24, no. 1: 1–12.

Duggan, Maeve, Nicole B. Ellison, Cliff Lampe, Amanda Lenhart, and Mary Madden. 2015. "Social Media Update 2014." Pew Research Center. January 9. http://www.pewinternet.org/2015/01/09/social-media-update-2014/.

Kotler, Philip, and Sidney J. Levy. 1969. "Broadening the Concept of Marketing." *Journal of Marketing* 33, no. 1: 10–15.

Nelson, Sandra. 2008. *Strategic Planning for Results.* Chicago: American Library Association.

Nicholson, Heather. 2014. "Tips from the Trenches: Marketing in a Small Pubic Library." *Feliciter* 60, no. 3 (June): 14–15.

Oldenburg, Ray. 1989. *The Great Good Place: Cafes, Coffee Shops, Community Centers, Beauty Parlors, General Stores, Bars, Hangouts and How They Get You through the Day.* New York: Paragon House.

Oliveira, Michael. 2013. "More Canadians Use Facebook Daily than Anywhere Else in the World," *Financial Post*, August 13. http://business.financialpost.com/2013/08/13/more-canadians-use-facebook-daily-than-anywhere-else-in-the-world/?__lsa=d324-0da2.

This chapter is an adapted and greatly expanded version of a previously published article (Nicholson, 2014).

Chapter Eleven

Library Programming

*Methods for Creation, Collaboration,
Delivery, and Outreach*

Amanda Piekart and
Bonnie Lafazan—Berkeley College Library

Library programming in itself *is* a best practice of library promotion and publicity. Creative and meaningful library programs promote and increase visibility of the library, its vast array of resources available including its knowledgeable librarians, and the opportunity to reach new library users. This chapter describes how Berkeley College librarians have used a creative and collaborative approach to programming to promote library services and programs.

BACKGROUND

Around 2009, there was an influx of several new librarians at Berkeley College, a four-year institution with ten separate locations in the tri-state area. These librarians brought fresh energy, innovation, and creative concepts that helped promote and increase the visibility of the Berkeley College Library. While the librarians *were* providing information literacy instruction for students in the classroom, it was the library's only method of outreach. During this period, Berkeley College's Student Development Department was primarily responsible for all student-centered programming. However, all of that changed with President Obama's Proclamation recognizing October as National Information Literacy Month (U.S. President, 2009). With this, Berkeley College librarians saw an opportunity to create unique and collaborative library programming. It was one of the first instances where the library collaborated with faculty, Student Development and Campus Life (hereafter "Student Development"), and librarians from other campus locations in a systemwide approach to present library programming beyond formal information literacy instruction. Some of the first programs for National Information Literacy Month included Social Networks as Information Sources, Wikipedia: Good or Evil, and Google Like a Guru. From thereon, a model of departmental collaboration shifted from delivering only information literacy instruction to implementing a large variety of original library programs. Some of those programs included Berkeley's Got Smarts; Everything You Need to Know about Social Reading in 10 Minutes; Library Media Olympics; How to Save and Share in the Cloud; Clue: A Library Mystery Game; Fifty Shades: Why So Much Buzz?; and National Poetry Month Poetry Reading.

We have learned that several components should be considered for library programming to flourish. Developing relationships; actively seeking out opportunities to collaborate; creating meaningful programs that instill learning; choosing appropriate delivery methods to reach diverse populations; considering necessary factors such as funding, time, staffing, and space; and assessing the event or activity to determine if the program was successful all play a crucial role in successful library programming.

DEVELOPING LIBRARY PROGRAMS

When developing library programs, Berkeley College librarians wanted to go beyond what the traditional classroom curriculum and library information literacy session typically offered to students. Because our objectives were to further encourage students to discover new interests while also inspiring them to become lifelong learners, the librarians began to explore other types of literacies, which included digital, consumer, and art and cultural literacies. In addition to focusing on various literacy skills, librarians' personal interests and tracking of trending topics were also factors in the development process.

Digital Literacy

Berkeley College librarians began to develop programs that encouraged digital literacy since it was a skill that was being newly defined and its importance was being recognized by library associations such as the American Library Association (ALA). In 2012, ALA defined digital literacy as "The ability to use information and communication technologies to find, evaluate, create, and communicate information, requiring both cognitive and technical skills" (ALA Digital Literacy Taskforce, 2012). Since the digital world is a major component of our daily lives, we believed that programs that addressed the use and understanding of technology would be practical and appealing to our users. A few examples of digital literacy programs created by Berkeley College librarians were Cool Productivity Apps, Web Browser Comparisons, Your Digital Footprint, and Current Technology Trends. Those who attended these programs found them to be useful for their personal, professional, and academic lives. Some comments from the Cool Productivity Apps program, for example, included "Great presentation! I will never use a flash drive again!—Thank You," "Excellent presentation! Very current and informative!" and "I downloaded some new apps you mentioned and I love them!"

Consumer Literacy

Another literacy we promoted that instills lifelong learning was consumer literacy. Consumer literacy programs were developed to bring awareness to library users on how they could become effective and deliberate when they are seeking, sharing, and using information. Programs promoting consumer literacy included Is Privacy Dead: A Forum on Privacy, Cybercondria: Where to Find Credible Medical Information, and How to Become a Smart Online Shopper.

Art and Cultural Literacy and Personal Interests

In many cases, the development of a program was driven by a librarian's personal interest. These programs were often the most successful since a librarian who was passionate about the subject would naturally put additional effort and time into promoting, preparing, and delivering his or her program. One example of a program driven by personal interest stemmed from a librarian's passion for art and culture; this program was Embracing the Zombie Apocalypse: Why We Are Obsessed with the End of the World. This program took a current trend in literature (dystopian novels, specifically zombies) and highlighted how zombies have been portrayed throughout history, in novels and art. After the program, this campus library experienced an increase in requests, checkouts, and purchase requests for zombie/apocalypse materials.

Another example is a poetry event that developed from a librarian's personal interest in poetry. After the first successful poetry event, several library theme-based poetry events were offered throughout the year during Halloween, Women's History Month, Black History Month, and National Poetry Month. During these poetry readings, students, librarians, faculty, and college staff read selected poems, discussed their meaning, and even shared their original poems. These events were easy to organize, strengthened the library's relationship with faculty, and provided users with exposure to different historical and cultural events.

Trending Topics

One final strategy that was implemented in order to promote Berkeley College Library resources and services was the creation of programs on trending topics. These types of programs were successful because we learned that with any trending topic, our community may only have a superficial understanding of that trend. One example of this type of program was a 3D printer webinar, which involved a short, ten-minute session highlighting the ten most important things someone should know about 3D printing. This program briefly explained what 3D printing was, how it was being used, and what the predictions were for its future uses. Another trending topic program hosted was Everything You Need to Know about E-Readers. These types of programs foster interest in learning something new and inspire users to be lifelong learners by demystifying a topic of interest for them and encouraging them to want to learn more. As you can see, when developing library programs, it's important to explore many different avenues that go beyond students' traditional classroom curricula and information literacy sessions. We included a variety of literacies, our librarians' personal interests, and trending topics in order to promote lifelong learning. Once we developed ideas for programs, the next challenge was to generate awareness and interest in the programs.

PROMOTING THE LIBRARY BEYOND THE LIBRARY WALLS

It took time to get these programs off the ground. Strategies used included attending other department's programs and participating in campuswide events, taking part in cross-departmental collaboration utilizing alternative delivery methods, and identifying diverse populations within Berkeley College.

Integrating with Campus Departments

One of the most successful strategies used was prominently establishing the librarians in the campus community, eventually becoming the face of our libraries. We learned that it was important to go beyond promoting services from our offices, behind the reference desk, or even just from within the library walls. By remaining in the library, interactions were limited to only those who physically came into the library. Additionally, the librarians wanted to be seen as much more than just people who help find books or assist with research questions. The librarians needed to be where the campus community was in order to develop relationships with faculty and students. Therefore, library staff started attending other department programs, such as car washes sponsored by a particular club, themed programs from Student

Development, job-searching workshops hosted by Career Services, and many more. Socializing outside the library with colleagues from other departments and students in an informal manner helped us become more attuned to campus interests. In addition to attending other department programs, library staff have also taken an active role in campuswide community service events and taken on advisory roles for student clubs. Over time, Berkeley College librarians were able to develop meaningful relationships that have opened the doors for cross-departmental collaborations.

Cross-Departmental Collaboration

Once these outside relationships were developed, it was easier to approach other departments with the intention to collaborate on planning and organizing events that would be beneficial to all, with a major goal of promoting and publicizing Berkeley College Library resources, personnel, and activities. Collaborating with other departments and student organizations has proven to be a great way to attract new audiences and, therefore, increase awareness and participation in library programs. Student Development has been a great resource since their primary role is to offer a diverse range of programs and activities to enhance the student experience. In most cases, they are able to provide the space, food, promotion, and audience. Librarians have also collaborated with the Academic Support Center on programs such as research writing workshops, where the library provided research support and the Academic Support Center provided writing support. For thematic programs, such as Domestic Violence Awareness Month sponsored by Student Counseling, the library has provided related books and other materials. Another department we have established an effective relationship with is Career Services. The library has collaborated with them on programs such as Job Searching Scams and How to Use the Internet to Find a Job. Another successful example of multidepartmental collaboration was a program held for National Information Literacy Awareness Month entitled OMG: Will Texting Destroy the Future of the English Language? This program included a panel discussion with representatives from Academic Support, Career Services, faculty, students, and the library.

Delivery Methods and Diverse Populations

Through collaborative efforts with other departments, Berkeley College librarians' interactions with the campus population increased. During this time, librarians realized that the programs created would not necessarily follow a "one size fits all" model. A variety of delivery methods needed to be developed to reach all of our users. These methods included short programs, social programs, weeklong programs, monthly programs, and webinars.

These methods also helped the library appeal to the college's diverse population. For example, for students who were short on time, librarians held ten-minute programs, such as Ten Things You Need to Know about Social Reading in Ten Minutes, or weeklong scavenger hunts that allowed students to complete the challenge when the time was right for them. For evening students, librarians participated in coffee meet-and-greets in a more social atmosphere. For gamers, we held chess tournaments or scavenger hunts. For college staff and faculty, the library hosted film and book clubs that met once a month or once a quarter. For online students, we hosted asynchronous online book clubs and webinars, such as Your Digital Footprint and Cool Websites and Apps.

The increased amount of programming along with better integration with the campus community has increased the opportunities to promote library services. The Berkeley College Library was now established as a department that encourages collaborative efforts and uses a wide range of delivery methods to reach all users through diverse programming.

FOUR KEY FACTORS FOR PLANNING A SUCCESSFUL PROGRAM

Once the librarians identified a program idea and reached out to the appropriate individual or department with which to collaborate, four factors were identified as being necessary for implementing your library program in order for it to be successful. The four factors were:

1. How much funds are needed?
2. How much time is required to develop the program?
3. What effect will this program have on staffing the library?
4. Where and when should we host the program?

Funding

When considering funding for your program, you should identify what resources are already available at your disposal, whether your program requires a prize incentive, and if it's possible to share funding costs with another department. Many programs may not call for any funding beyond the use of the supplies that are already available (e.g., copy paper, markers, tape, glue, etc.). Use existing supplies to make flyers or creative displays to post physically in key locations around campus, but advertise virtually with free Web services as well, to support and promote upcoming library programs.

Prize incentives should usually be reserved for games or scavenger hunt programs. For most programs that offer a prize, use college memorabilia, such as shirts, coffee mugs, flash drives, or book bags. Perhaps your college bookstore will donate items or offer them at a discounted rate. Students love these types of prizes, especially because they are useful and they also help instill school spirit and pride.

Last but not least, when collaborating with other departments or organizations, see if any expenses, even minor ones, can be shared among the cohosting groups or departments. For example, because of the shared departmental expenses, you may wish to offer food or refreshments. Food is a great way to entice people to sign up and participate in a program.

Time

Another factor to consider when developing programs is how long it will take to create and launch each program. Many of the programs were one-shot sessions, while others occurred over days, weeks, or months. Librarians had to discover time-efficient ways to make the development of all of these new programs more manageable as the planning, program preparation, and collaborating needed to be accomplished in addition to librarians' existing duties.

The type of program being offered usually determined how much time was needed for development. When it comes to some of the shorter programs, such as the ten-minute programs and webinars, it usually requires about one to two weeks of development time. For a one-shot program, time preparation varies between two weeks to one month. Other programs that span the course of a week—or even multiple weeks—were not only a time commitment of at least two to three months during the developmental stage, but they were also a time commitment while the program was running.

Library staff have found that using templates, sharing resources, and reviving previous programs have all served as great time-saving practices. Librarians have used templates that are freely available online, such as a Jeopardy Game template. Once the template has been created, the game content could be altered based on the theme of the program. For example, Jeopardy questions can be easily altered for Black History Month or library trivia. Another idea is to share existing presentations, handouts, and activities from successful programs between librarians within your library department. For example, one librarian created Clue: A Library Mystery Game, a successful event held during Information Literacy Month. All material (presentation, handouts, and clues) were shared with other librarians so that they could implement it at their own campus library. Finally, reviving past programs and events that occur annually, such as National Women's History Month, can also serve as a time-saving practice, especially during preparation.

Finally, seeking out opportunities to collaborate is a great solution to making the development process of these programs less time consuming and more manageable. Collaborating with other colleagues (internally or with other departments) has many benefits, including reducing the workload of a program and sharing resources. Whether it is creating the flyer, securing a location, notifying appropriate college staff, or even developing the program itself, collaboration has been a successful solution to reducing a librarian's individual time commitment to a program.

Staffing

Staffing is yet another consideration when planning and conducting library events. How will the event affect the operations of the library? Will the program take place within existing work hours, and if so, can the library be adequately staffed while the program is being conducted?

While Berkeley College Library job descriptions indicate that advocating library services and participating in campus and collegewide events are librarians' responsibilities, any programs created and initiated by the librarians are considered above and beyond regular day-to-day activities and job duties. Therefore, since we have to make sure that the library operates as usual, staffing must always be considered. Most of the time, these programs were held during normally scheduled work hours with minimal disruption to staff schedules. However, there were some instances when classes were targeted to participate in library programs during normal work hours, where minor adjustments in staffing had to be made, or where additional coverage support was coordinated in advance.

It was important to inform all library staff of upcoming programs ahead of time because staff need to be able to promote the event and even encourage users to sign up. This can be best accomplished through e-mail and in-person explanations of the programs. Explanation of a program was as simple as sharing the flyer or as complex as explaining how much assistance library staff are allowed to give students if they are participating in a scavenger hunt.

Space

The last consideration was finding an optimal space to host the program. The space that you select for your program will depend on your need to access technology, such as computers or projectors, the anticipated number of attendees, and determining if your library is the optimal space for the program. If your program is hands-on and requires the use of several computers and your library cannot accommodate this, then you must look for other locations, such as a computer or classroom lab. When Berkeley librarians host a program and invite several classes, a larger alternative space must be found, such as the Student Center or the auditorium.

On some Berkeley College campuses, the library is not very visible, and in order to increase awareness, librarians have held their programs in the Student Center or in another location that might receive the most foot traffic. On other campuses, the library is in an ideal, central location and, therefore, is always used for hosting a successful program. However, the library might not be an optimal space for your program regardless of attendees or visibility. For live webinars, it was important to find a space that would be the least disruptive to students but was also a quiet space that would allow the presenter to be heard by all viewers.

THREE SUCCESSFUL PROGRAMS

Now that we have explained the importance of developing an idea, getting involved in your campus community, seeking out opportunities to collaborate, and determining important factors to consider in planning and presenting a program, the next part of this chapter shares how these strategies work together and were utilized during three successful programs: Library Media Olympics, the Traveling Librarian Tours, and a three-part technology series.

Library Media Olympics

The idea for Library Media Olympics grew out of the interest and buzz around the 2012 Summer Olympics. A group of librarians from different campuses had a conversation about incorporating some type of contest or program around the theme of the Olympics but wanted to be sure it would directly relate to library resources and services. Since it was summer, and students and college staff generally had more time, it seemed like a fun idea to encourage reading books and watching movies. The librarians discussed and developed the rules for the contest: if a participant read a book, they received one point; if they watched a movie, they received one point; and if they both read the book and watched the movie the book was based on, they received two points for each item. Students were to turn in their tracking booklets as soon as they were complete and then could pick up another blank booklet. Finally, as a learning tool and incentive to use and contribute to the library catalog, participants were encouraged to write a review of an item they read or watched for a total of three points for the review. Essentially, a participant could receive ten points total if they read a book, watched the movie that was based on the book, and reviewed both of them in the library catalog.

The participant who read the most books and watched the most movies would win the campus contest, and the campus library with the highest overall score would be the systemwide winner. In order to make it an even more exciting competition, librarians pitched the idea to all the library directors so that it could be a systemwide competition, and six campus libraries agreed to participate. The librarians then worked together to collaborate on standardized signage, outreach materials, and contest booklets. Funding for promotional materials were minimal or at no cost for those campuses who already had existing poster board and colored paper. While there was a lot of preparation needed for this event, the burden was not on one person since more than ten librarians collaborated on this program. In addition to the standardized signage, some campuses also created library displays of movies and the books that those movies were based on in order to promote the contest. Others posted materials on how to create an account in the library catalog and post a review for an item. Once the program was rolled out, posters were displayed in each library with the updated weekly tally of results.

Interest in the program was high because participants were excited about the ease of reading books and watching movies for entertainment purposes and potentially getting rewarded for it. Besides promoting library services and resources, this program encouraged critical thinking skills, writing skills, and a variety of lifelong learning skills through gaining knowledge of literature, cultural arts, and film. The program also reached a diverse population because some participants were avid readers and others were movie watchers. Not only did students participate, but faculty and college staff did as well. It also reached new users, who normally might not attend or participate in a program because of the time or scheduled elements. The program spanned over twelve weeks, so that everyone was able to participate on their own time. As the weeks progressed and the campus numbers were posted, each campus began to rally to encourage current participants and recruit new participants to read and watch more. With the increase of awareness and recruitment of new participants, librarians were collecting booklets and updating the poster scoreboard daily. Although it may seem like it would have been a huge burden on the library director to be updating the information daily, it was not, because all staff (full-time, part-time, and even student workers) were trained on how to keep the tallies updated. Because of the library's relationship with Student Development, they were more than happy to utilize their budget so that the winning campus was able to have their pizza party in the Student Center. The library was also able to reduce the cost of funds needed by purchasing prizes for the individual winners at a discounted rate from the bookstore. This program proved to have great value to the library as participants gained a new appreciation for the library staff and resources. While this program had been mostly perceived as academic in nature, the contest itself instilled an exciting entertainment value to literacy and learning.

The success of the Library Media Olympics program was very easy to assess since the goal of the program was so participation focused. In addition to the number of participants, staff tracked the types of users who participated, the most popular books and movies checked out, and the days and times participation was highest. During the course of this program, we learned that students were mostly checking out DVDs, and college staff were mainly checking out fiction materials. This information allowed us to target the college staff in the future when it came to purchasing and promoting the fiction collection. To date, this program has been the library's most successful program, with 154 participants.

Traveling Librarian Tours

The idea for the Traveling Librarians developed from librarians at one campus whose library is located in the lower level or basement of a building, so the library is not immediately visible to the students and staff. The librarians decided to fill a rolling book cart with new books and other materials that would be of interest and travel around campus to faculty and staff offices, student lounges, and computer labs. An untapped user audience was reached by an unexpected visit from the librarians with their book cart. The librarians found that staff and students were enthusiastic about checking out books, interested in knowing if certain books were available, and inquired about items they wished to put on hold. Many expressed that they had not utilized the library prior to the traveling book cart because they had not thought to visit the library, or had no time to visit; some were embarrassed to admit they did not know that a library actually existed on campus.

The Traveling Librarians program successfully brought together many of the suggestions dealing with funding, time, staffing, and space mentioned earlier in this chapter, with new library users and new relationships formed during each tour. As far as funding, there was none required, which essentially made the program free outreach for the library. While not much preparation was required, adequate planning was essential. Time required for the program was in the scheduling of the tours and during tours themselves. The tours were scheduled four times quarterly, taking into consideration times where there would be users on campus and considering staff coverage of the library during the tours. The tours themselves ranged from thirty minutes to one hour, depending on the amount of interactions and time spent with users. As far as staffing, the most important element was scheduling in advance so that the library had adequate coverage. Sometimes just one librarian would go on a tour, sometimes two. If one librarian went on tour, a time-saving practice was to have the other librarian or student worker prepare the cart of new and interesting materials, due date cards, and a small laptop for tracking checkouts and requests. Statistics were taken on how many users were reached, how many materials were checked out, how many holds were placed, and how many requests were made to purchase new items. Other campuses followed suit and held weekly or quarterly traveling librarian tours on their campuses. The Traveling Librarian Tours provided excellent opportunities for collaborations, conversations, and on-the-spot learning. By utilizing a small laptop with wireless connection, some participants learned how to use the library catalog and place materials on hold for the first time, while others learned how to access e-books from their public libraries. These skills incorporated digital literacy and promoted lifelong learning

Our Traveling Librarian Tours, which have occurred across four campuses now, have provided fruitful information. At one campus, the librarians would request that college employees fill out short surveys so that the next time the rolling book cart came around, it was loaded with more material that supported their interests and, therefore, increased the likelihood of future checkouts. The Traveling Librarian Tours have continuously proven to be one of the best programs to date, not to mention a free outreach program, directly supporting the library's mission and promoting its materials and services.

Three-Part Technology Series

A three-part technology series began as a one-shot workshop, entitled "Productivity Tools and Apps for the College Student," which was offered during New Student Orientation Week at one Berkeley College campus location. The students expressed so much interest in this program and related ideas that the librarians and the Student Development director decided to work together to expand this offering, developing three new workshops for the following quarter. The three-part technology series, entitled Free Productivity Apps and Websites for the College Student, consisted of three workshops: "Part 1: Cloud Computing from Anywhere"; "Part 2: Cool Free Apps and Websites You Should Know About"; and "Part 3: Websites for Your Personal Life." Technology, consumer literacy, and critical thinking skills were all embedded into the various workshops.

The three-part technology series also considered the four necessary factors (funding, time, staffing, and space) as well as the best practices mentioned earlier in this chapter. The program required no additional funding beyond the use of existing supplies and printers in order to create the handouts, certificates, and surveys. Student Development agreed to use their budget to host a lunch for the final workshop and three-part certificate ceremony. A huge undertaking of time was required to develop and create the three-part series. While one part was revived from the new student orientation program, the other two parts had to be created from scratch. Luckily, two librarians collaborated on the development of these workshops, which helped reduce the preparation time. Each workshop, which included the creation of the presentation, handouts, and an assessment component, took approximately two to four weeks to develop. The workshops were held monthly for one and a half hours each. Since these programs were created well in advance of their offering, we were able to ensure adequate staffing and coverage of the library. Because of planning and timing, both librarians were able to be present at all three workshops, in addition to having coverage to support the library itself.

The optimal space for this workshop was not the library, since we did not wish to interrupt library services. Through the library's collaboration with Student Development, we were able to reserve the Student Center for all three workshops. Not only was there increased visibility of the program in the Student Center, as it is a prime location at that campus, the space also provided the necessary technology for the presentation along with comfortable chairs and seating for participants.

In order to reach a diverse population, the library reached out to faculty to bring their classes to the programs. Additionally, with Student Development promoting the program to their captive audience, they were able to reach students the librarians may not have necessarily been able to reach. The success of this program would not have been possible without faculty and Student Development collaboration and participation; the Student Development director provided the food and space, while certain faculty members required their students to attend.

Each workshop had a pre-assessment, a post-assessment, and a survey to help ensure that learning outcomes were met. The survey asked questions that would allow librarians to see what was and was not working, what hours would work best to run the program again, and any other comments that may be helpful for future similar programs. When the participants were asked questions related to teaching style, program length, participation incentives, best locations, and so on, library staff took that information into consideration when developing future programs, using highly recommended free services like Poll Everywhere or Doodle, or inexpensive tools such as Survey Monkey. All of the technologies taught (e.g., Mozilla Popcorn, Prezi) in the workshops were also highly rated and free and specifically used as much as possible within the sessions in order to best demonstrate their use and appeal. As an added incentive, students received certificates at each program and were encouraged to add the workshops to their résumé under skills following completion of the workshop. Students who attended all three workshops received a special certificate at the final workshop.

The three-part technology series was an excellent example of program development that instilled learning (i.e., technology literacy), built relationships (with attendees, librarians, and faculty) and collaboration (Student Development staff and librarians), utilized best practices (funding, time, staffing, and space), and promoted library services and personnel—in fact, many students who attended these technology programs later came back to the library seeking out the librarians for their services or simply to follow up about cool new apps or cloud computing tools they had learned.

CONCLUSION

Since its inception, the library's fresh approach to programming has opened many doors, built new relationships across Berkeley College, and dramatically increased participation from the campus community. Library programming can be used to support any of your services; however, having a successful program entails more than just developing an idea for a meaningful program. You must consider your audience, seek out opportunities to collaborate with other departments, and carefully plan your program by addressing four key factors as outlined in this chapter. Becoming integrated into your community will not only allow you to become more in tune with your campus community's interests and instill lifelong learning, but it will also allow you to build relationships with other departments, which will then lead to collaboration. Collaboration (internal or external) will not only raise awareness about your programs and, therefore, your services, but it will also assist with the tasks of finding the funding, time, staffing, and space needed to plan and present successful programs. As we have learned from experience, it is imperative to assess every program. When you are assessing, you should consider the program's purpose, success, skills taught, and the value of continuing the program. Reflecting on these aspects of library programming will drive future planning. The strategies developed for creation, delivery, and outreach for library programming will continue to be an essential component of promoting the Berkeley College library staff, resources, and events.

REFERENCES

ALA Digital Literacy Task Force. 2012. "Digital Literacy Definition." American Library Association. http://connect.ala.org/node/181197.

U.S. President. 2009. "National Information Literacy Awareness Month, 2009, Proclamation 8429." *Federal Register* 74, no. 193 (October 7): 51445. http://www.gpo.gov/fdsys/pkg/FR-2009-10-07/pdf/E9-24290.pdf.

Chapter Twelve

"Flipping the Switch" for School Library Advocacy

Sara Kelly Johns—School Librarian and Speaker/Consultant on School Library Advocacy

INTRODUCTION

When the American Association of School Librarians (AASL) published *Empowering Learners: Guidelines for School Library Media Programs*, the guidelines for school librarian practice, in 2009, a fifth role for school librarians was added to the four more familiar roles (teacher, information specialist, instructional partner, program administrator). The new role was *leadership*, and the guidelines describe the need to be vision-headed, to build collaborative relationships, and to be interactive within and outside the school (AASL, 2009). The guidelines include: "The school library media program is guided by an advocacy plan that builds support from decision makers who affect the quality of the [school library media program]" (AASL, 2009: 41).

Advocacy must be part of the job description for school librarians; a personal commitment is not optional. Advocacy for school librarians has two fronts—program advocacy and legislative advocacy—and both are important. A school library program within a library with its doors shut is no longer acceptable. The goal of teaching students who are creative, love to learn, and have the dispositions to be skillful users of information, who graduate "college and career ready," is not done in isolation.

Partnering with the school community and professional organizations means being active when library-related legislation needs support—the legislative advocacy that is part of that leadership role.

It is crucial for school librarians to have a good school library program tied to the mission and curriculum of the school. However, promotion and marketing must be part of that program. With a nod to Jim Collins's *Good to Great* (2001), it is not a *great* school library program if no one knows about it. A solid marketing and promotion plan provides the visibility and support that will lead to school library advocates.

In a 2008 *Teacher Librarian* article, an "offensive formula" is presented that helps school librarians establish their programs, facility, and themselves as indispensable to their school's mission. In the article's formula, $P + M = A$, the "variables" are **P**romotion and **M**arketing equals a cohort of **A**dvocates, those people who are ready to support and advance your school library program with decision makers (Johns, 2008: 36). This cohort springs into action when there is a threat to cut staff or budget in the school library; a parent in such a cohort could write a letter to the editor or an op-ed, make a phone call to a school administrator or board member, perhaps show up at a board budget hearing when mobilized. Students, teachers, and community members make phone calls to or e-mail local, state, and federal legislators when legislation can strengthen school libraries—but they need to understand and value the contributions that school librarians and strong library programs make to student learning.

That does not just happen—it takes reflection and planning by school librarians to develop a promotion and marketing plan (referred to hereafter as a marketing plan) that will be effective in their own workplace. School librarians work best for legislative advocacy by cooperating with professional organizations as discussed below, but although professional organizations often offer excellent resources, no one is going to develop a boilerplate marketing plan for the school librarian; it must be done individually to make a difference. Building a personal core of advocates/champions needs to be deliberate and continual, the ultimate result of a carefully crafted marketing plan.

School librarians are often not comfortable with promotion and marketing but need to "get over it" and realize that it's about their programs—not them—and develop a promotion and marketing plan to fit their situation and needs. During an interview with *Library Girl* blog author Jennifer LaGarde where she described losing 50 percent of her library paraprofessional's services despite having a stellar school library program, she described the realization that, not only did she need to have a collaborative program that results in students who are college and career ready, those students, her teachers, her administrators, her parents, and her community need to know what she does to reach that goal and why it matters. For instance, explaining to students *why* they are learning lifelong information literacy skills as well as *how* to do an effective search can result in students who are among your biggest advocates. Like Jennifer, all school librarians, must "flip the switch" to be aware, active leaders for advocacy (LaGarde, 2013a).

SCHOOL LIBRARY ADVOCACY: DEFINITIONS

The definitions on the AASL advocacy website (http://www.ala.org/aasl/advocacy/definitions) demonstrate the differences between advocacy, marketing, and promotion clearly. The differences need to be considered before developing a personal marketing plan:

> **Advocacy:** On-going process of building partnerships so that others will act for and with you, turning passive support into educated action for the library program. It begins with a vision and a plan for the library program that is then matched to the agenda and priorities of stakeholders.
>
> **Public Relations (PR):** One-way communication of getting the message across: who we are, what we do, when and where, and for whom.
>
> **Marketing:** A planned and sustained process to assess the customer's needs and then to select materials and services to meet those needs. You must know the customer's needs, who they are, what they need, when and where you can best deliver it, and what you are willing to pay. (AASL, 2015)

DEVELOPING A MARKETING PLAN

These somewhat generic definitions lead school librarians to begin planning by reflecting on: vision, mission, goals, objectives, characteristics/perceptions of school libraries, target audiences (internal and external), messaging, and visibility. Over a decade ago, AASL and other divisions of the American Library Association (ALA) developed the @your library Campaign for America's Libraries (http://www.ala.org/advocacy/advleg/publicawareness/campaign@yourlibrary/), which resulted in the first widespread tool kit for developing marketing/communications plans in school libraries (ALA, 2010a). A nationwide campaign with national and state training introduced these professionally designed tools and approach to many school librarians, who then faced their challenges armed with a plan—a marketing plan—for the first time. It is no longer unusual for students in library schools to develop an advocacy plan as part of one of their courses, such as in Debra Kachel's course "School Library Advocacy" at Mansfield University's School Library and Information Technologies Online Master's Program.

Although the AASL *@your library Toolkit* was published in 2003, most of it is quite relevant today (ALA, 2003). The ALA divisions have continued to update their advocacy materials to keep the above classic process current. In 2008, then ALA president Camila Alire developed an initiative for "frontline advocacy" (http://www.ala.org/advocacy/advleg/advocacyuniversity/

frontline_advocacy) that targets development of effective messaging for the internal audience, the staff, including frontline advocacy for school libraries. Providing tools for such techniques as SWOT (strengths, weaknesses, opportunities, and threats) analysis, this process leads school librarians through simple tools and strategies to develop the "A-team" of anyone who works for or is passionate about their school library and makes advocacy part of their everyday conversation and activities—librarians, staff, volunteers, and administrators. Including this process in a school library marketing plan makes it accepted by more of the school library community (ALA, 2010b).

More recently, the AASL and the Association of Library Service to Children (ALSC), divisions of ALA, have made strong, recently updated advocacy tools available. AASL and ALA have developed a school library campaign (http://ilovelibraries.org) targeting the public, "School Libraries Make a Difference," which includes such marketing tools as guidelines for writing an op-ed. ALSC's "Everyday Advocacy" campaign provides tools to craft and deliver messages, including use of electronic media (http://www.ala.org/everyday-advocacy/speak-out/electronic-media).

While there are many models for developing a marketing plan, using the school-library-targeted steps from the AASL *@your library Toolkit* (ALA, 2003: 15–16), along with frontline advocacy tools, what does the process of developing a school or district school library marketing plan look like? It starts with reflection—a vision and a mission statement.

Vision and Mission Statement

As school librarians start their work on a marketing plan, a vision of what your library will be in the future is the very first step. An example from the school library in Lee Magnet High School in Baton Rouge, Louisiana, documents aspirations for the library:

"The Lee High School Library Media Center prepares dynamic learners in an information rich environment to be resourceful, reflective, and responsible readers and users of information" (Luther, 2015).

While a vision statement is what you want to achieve—a big "reach"—a mission statement for your school library program supports the district or school's mission statement through the unique values to the school of a strong school library program. Language needs to be concise and simple; the mission statement needs to be short. Can you capture what your library does in one sentence? Can you recite it easily? What does your library do that makes it indispensable to the students in your school?

AASL recently updated the organization's mission statement, which can be adapted for any school or district because it focuses not on school libraries but on student learning, important for credibility in the school community: "The American Association of School Librarians empowers leaders to transform teaching and learning" (AASL, 2014). "The _____ School Library transforms teaching and learning" is concise; the verb "transforms" is powerful and sends a positive message.

Stacey Luther at Lee High School Library Media Center developed the mission statement below that complements her vision statement:

> The mission of the Lee High School Library and Media Center is to foster the development of information literate students who are effective users of ideas and information and become lifelong independent learners.
>
> The Lee High School Library and Media Center is at the heart of the learning community, providing resources, programs, learning opportunities, and support for the academic and personal interests of the students.
>
> The Lee High School Library offers open access to students and the school librarians collaboratively plan with teachers to formulate student centered, resource-based learning activities that support the curriculum and promote recreational reading. (Luther, 2015)

Jennifer Jamison, school librarian in the Atlantic City School District, realized that a school district marketing plan would move school libraries forward for the district's students. Jennifer worked for two years on her plan and, together with her superintendent, brought it successfully to the school board for their approval for the entire district (Jamison, 2015). Jamison's plan begins with the school district libraries' student-centered mission statement: "The mission of our Atlantic City Public Schools' libraries is to prepare our students to be college and career ready by providing students equal access to digital and print resources, literacy programs, and current technology, which are integrated into the curriculum" (Atlantic City High School, 2014).

Goals

Now that you have a vision and mission statement, what are your goals? What do you want to happen? School librarians are teachers and thus are familiar with SMART goals: **S**pecific, **M**easurable, **A**ttainable, **R**ealistic, and **T**imed (Haughey, 2014).

The goals in the Atlantic City School District libraries are SMART goals:

1. Increase visibility through development of social media, web management system and e-mail.
2. Spread the vision of school libraries through parent and community outreach.
3. Increase our voice.
4. Be vigilant at spreading what school libraries are doing.
5. Increase student involvement. (Atlantic City High School, 2014)

Each of those goals is listed with one to three objectives that demonstrate the "Objectives" step of the AASL @*your library Toolkit*, the next step in plan development. An example for the first goal is to create portal access to library resources by utilizing the Library E-Chalk database page and Destiny online catalog page. Another example (for goal 4) is to stream into classrooms a quarterly infomercial about a book review, school library resource, or an event happening in the library. Goal 5, student involvement, includes an objective to host game nights and community reads.

Positioning Statement

A next step in the AASL @*your library Toolkit* is to define a positioning statement, how you communicate the value of your school library. How do you want the library to be perceived? How would you define the image you would like for your library? Your messaging language and its match to your "target" needs are factors that evaluate your positioning statement.

Barbara Stripling states that the characteristics of school libraries need to be streamlined: "Our audience need simplicity; they do not want to hear all the complexities about each aspect of a school library program. . . . By defining the major areas of impact of a library program and describing them in simple language, we were trying to open a conversation between librarians and their communities about the values that a library brings to the community it serves" (Stripling, 2014: 11). Stripling is referring to her ALA presidential initiative the "Declaration for the Right to Libraries" (http://www.ala.org/advocacy/declaration-right-libraries) and, especially relevant to a school library marketing plan, the "Declaration for the Right to School Libraries" (http://www.ala.org/advocacy/school-library-month-focuses-declaration-right-school-libraries).

As one answers the question again and again, "Why do we need school libraries when we have Google?" it is easy to find the positive messages needed in a school library marketing plan by looking at statements from the "Declaration for the Right to School Libraries":

School libraries change lives.
School libraries empower the individual.
School libraries support literacy and lifelong learning.
School libraries strengthen families.
School libraries are the great equalizer.
School libraries build communities.
School libraries protect our right to know.
School libraries strengthen our nation.
School libraries advance research and scholarship.
School libraries help us to better understand each other.
School libraries preserve our nation's cultural heritage. (ALA, 2013)

Key Messaging: Stripling

The school library's key message needs to be on the tip of the tongue for every member of the school community; developing that message is the purpose of the frontline advocacy initiative described above. Involving all staff—librarians, clerks, teachers, students, administrators, secretaries—in the messaging means that all those people are advocates for school library programming. That strategy can result in a brand, a list of talking points, and even a hashtag for the school library.

Stripling also shares her findings about communicating the value of school libraries. She, along with the rest of the school library community, knows that the results of the more than sixty correlational studies done in the United States and Canada demonstrate the impact of the school librarian on student learning. However, Stripling acknowledges that, to have an impact, it is crucial to back up national and state research with local action research, to "develop qualitative measures through surveys, conversations, interviews and self-assessment instruments [to] add depth to the local advocacy messages" . . . and to collect stories (Stripling, 2014: 11).

Key Messaging: Kowalski

Sue Kowalski, middle school librarian at Pine Grove Middle School in East Syracuse, New York, faced two years of working out of a library space the size of a classroom and teaching collaboratively for student instruction with teachers spread out between the district's six other schools while a new middle school was being built. She not only bought "Miss Lindy," a used camper, to outfit as a "bookmobile," she evaluated her library program for its actions (investments) and their impact (payoffs), using the results to craft the messages for her temporary program (Kowalski, 2015). Sue's full results are available on the author's wiki (http://frugalschoollibrarian.wikispaces.com/home).

Key Messaging: Buerkett

Action research conducted by Rebecca Buerkett, district librarian in the Tupper Lake (New York) Central School District, clearly shows the impact of her position being realigned to cover both the elementary and high school libraries after the retirement of the high school librarian; she had previously been the school librarian for the elementary school only. In a spreadsheet, Buerkett documented the difference in her instruction for the elementary students between December 2013 when she was in the single position and in December 2014 when she covered both schools. Buerkett let the data speak for itself; the middle/high school principal was very concerned that the fifth and sixth graders were not going to be prepared when they reached his school

(Buerkett, 2015). A second school library position was included in the following year's budget.

Target Audiences

The AASL *@your library Toolkit* lists the key internal and external audiences that need to be identified as the next step. Internal audiences include staff, student assistants, and volunteers; external audiences include teachers, administrators, students, parents, board of education members, community members, prospective partners, and media. Not only are these groups targeted by the goals and objectives, they are the potential members of a cohort of advocates. As they better understand the value of the school librarian and the school library program, they are more likely to become someone who will write that letter to the editor or make that phone call when support is needed. An amusing example was the principal's wife, who substituted in the school library while the librarian was at a library conference. When the librarian returned, the woman told her that, when she was a social studies teacher in another town, she always thought the easiest two jobs in the school were the principal and the school librarian. Now she was married to a principal and had substituted for the librarian and knew how wrong she was. Perceptions!

Jennifer LaGarde in her *Library Girl* blog shared a graphic (see figure 12.1) that outlines an action plan for changing perceptions about the value of school libraries, including reflection on which work done by school librarians no longer needs to be done (LaGarde, 2013b).

After developing her mission, goals and objectives, and key messages, Atlantic City's Jennifer Jamison identified key groups as part of her marketing plan and developed strategies to deliver her message to her stakeholders, excerpted below:

1. Monthly breakfasts and lunches in the elementary buildings for teachers, highlighting one thing to share in three minutes or less. Examples included making resource lists for students or demonstrating a new iPad app.
2. Published a monthly S'more/Newsletter that highlights concepts that would appeal to all grade levels (i.e., using informational text, etc.).
3. Developed a handbook of policies, forms, and library services that teachers kept on their desks next to the contact list for the building.
4. Presented at board meetings, convinced and worked with administrators to get policies and procedures approved by the board for the district (i.e., all school libraries in Atlantic City would have a flexible schedule, etc.). (Jamison, 2015)

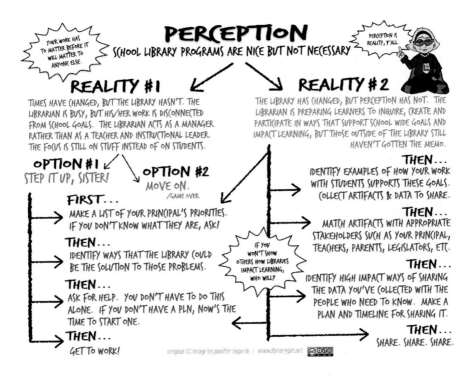

Figure 12.1. *Library Girl* blog: Perceptions of School Library Programs graphic.

Strategies for Delivering the Messages

An important step in a marketing plan is identifying all ways of communicating your message, then focusing both on the most effective methods for you and those that need immediate attention. This is where good public relations strategies are important. Methods can include such traditional ones as flyers, bookmarks, banners, posters, displays, press releases, and e-mail messages, but increasingly social media. Rebecca Buerkett, for instance, uses a school Twitter account followed by her teachers and administration and some of her students to share information about library events and new technology applications targeted to her audience.

For school librarians who have not been involved with the media (newspapers, radio, television), the AASL *@your library Toolkit* (ALA, 2003) provides templates and advice for being interviewed, advising school librarians to work with their district's public relations staff or district administration to make allies for impactful PR. Another excellent resource for PR and communications help is Margaux DelGuidice and Rose Luna's *Make a Big Impact at Your School Board Meeting* (DelGuidice and Luna, 2012).

In Jennifer Jamison's marketing plan, she targeted updating the libraries' Web pages, which are often the face of the library for students, teachers, and parents. Resources and messages are available 24/7. She utilized the website template in Joyce Valenza's *Power Tools Recharged* (Valenza, 2004) for all the schools to get their start.

School libraries are often restricted to the interfaces used by the school district, although some develop their own websites as a link from the school's library Web page. Jamison's Web page (http://achs.acboe.org/site_res_view_folder.aspx?id=b12bb913-807a-4bd3-8305-86676ff0902e) now reflects the elements in Valenza's template with several subpages. She and Sue Kowalski (http://pinegrove.libguides.com/home?hs=a) have developed a series of LibGuides to deliver resources for students' instruction virtually, a widely used format for school librarians. A "coup" for school librarians is getting the link to their library Web page on the front page of the school website, instead of a listing as a subpage under "Academics" or "Student Services."

Elissa Malespina, supervisor of technology at the Parsippany Troy Hills (New Jersey) Board of Education, presents frequently on the use of social media to market a school library and shared a link to her keynote presentation in a private Facebook message (Malespina, 2015). Working within the district's social media policies (though school librarians can greatly influence these by having a relevant and learning-centered social media presence), school librarians push out their messaging using Twitter, Facebook (including targeting parents and the community), Animoto, Instagram, Pinterest (used as a curation tool for student projects), blogs, and much more. In 2011, Rebecca Ekstrom, librarian at Algonquin Middle School in Averill Park, New York, organized the many photos she took of student activities in the school library into a quarterly report using the Web-based Animoto. She hoped that she would get the attention of her principal—and she did. He sent it on to the superintendent and, shortly, the Animoto (https://animoto.com/play/X1hw2PN3KSFa9atIR9SPRw) was linked to on the district website's front page as an example of the learning that happens in Averill Park School District.

The previously mentioned ALSE "Everyday Advocacy" initiative includes a subpage on speaking out that gives sound guidelines on the use of electronic media for marketing and advocacy and is helpful for those who are using it professionally for the first time. It's also a good review for school librarians who want to add Facebook, Twitter, Tumblr, or Pinterest to their current social media outreach (ALSC, 2014).

A creative example of a school librarian who is consciously and deliberately targeting the messages of instructional collaboration and a strong school library program to the teachers in her school came in a personal communication from Katharine St. Laurent, school librarian at Solvay (New York) High School:

> I did my orientations with an eye toward teachers. The goal was to let students know about library services, but I also had the opportunity to educate the entire English department. I'm thinking of doing the orientation through a different department each year so that all teachers eventually see my spiel.
>
> I'm also the queen of "targeted librarian-ing." I have a mental catalog of each teacher's interests and curriculum and I'm on the lookout 24/7 for things that might help. Not super-efficient but it is appreciated and helps build relationships.
>
> I also volunteered to compile the school's weekly newsletter because (1) it makes me useful to the principal, (2) it keeps me in the loop with happenings in the building and (3) I can advertise library services as much as I want. (St. Laurent, 2015)

Visibility

A crucial piece of school library marketing is visibility—which leads to credibility and trust of the school library program and the school librarians in a district. Jennifer Jamison's experiences marketing her library program "flipped the advocacy switch" within her school district. However, not only should school librarians be seen within the school (but outside the library) at faculty and curriculum meetings and as part of important committee meetings, it is important to be visible and involved in school and community events such as sporting events, concerts, festivals, and plays.

One outstanding example of marketing the school library to the community is Books on Bikes in Charlottesville, Virginia, which markets the role of school libraries and encouragement of reading through a community outreach program created by two school librarians. Rebecca Flowers, school librarian at Walker Upper Elementary School, always wanted to drive a bookmobile, and when she and Mary Craig, Clark Elementary School librarian, invited themselves to a community event to help children get ready for school, they had such a great time handing out books and bookmarks that they decided to create a bookmobile at a scale they could handle, Books on Bikes (http://booksonbikescville.org/). Together with Clark Elementary third grade teacher Kelly Keyser, they created a Kickstarter project to buy rugged bikes and more books after their first summer (2013) of using their own bikes and a wagon to distribute books to children in low-income areas.

With the Kickstarter funding, they are now able to bring engaging, award-winning books and popsicles to students twice a week all summer. They kick off the summer of reading with a parade from one of the schools to a nearby public library to connect children with the summer reading program, increasing the children's comfort level at the public library and access to reading.

Often that comfort reaches the parents as well, opening up the resources of the public library to people who might not always take advantage of the riches available in the public libraries.

At the end of the summer, they end with Books on a Bus. On the last delivery day of the summer, they use a school bus filled with teachers and school administrators. Visiting all seven neighborhoods in one evening (instead of one to three a day on bikes), teachers visit the neighborhoods of their students. Seeing their teachers in their neighborhood is often one of the most exciting parts of the evening for the kids. Teachers see former students and meet students that will be in their classrooms in the new school year. It's another opportunity to connect schools with students, parents, and the community. Flowers and Craig find that the summer's efforts reach their community and their school district, focusing attention on the value of school libraries in support of children's literacy. Most of all, students show up in the fall with a personal connection to the library, excited about reading and talking about their books. The students use the library more often and take out more books, while the school library's active leadership for literacy is visible to the community, the school district, and the parents (Flowers, 2015).

EVALUATION MEASURES

Assessment of the impact of a marketing plan on a school library program is not clear-cut. How will you know what worked and what didn't? School librarians can collect pre- and post-data for such actions as increasing the number of collaborative units designed with teachers, the number of students accessing the library Web page, or the use of such resources as databases and books. Surveys of colleagues, verbally or formally via a print or online survey tools, can help school librarians identify successes or gaps to plan the next steps. Retention of positions or the addition of paraprofessional staff are very public successes.

Anecdotal evidence of the school library's value to the district and community is also a valid assessment. Jennifer Jamison, for instance, after the development and districtwide acceptance of the marketing plan she worked on for two years, is now at the district's high school, moved from an elementary position. Jamison has been successful in securing a Laura Bush Grant for school resources and putting together the top People's Choice–winning video for the recent Follett Challenge. Because of the marketing plan, the library program is strong and healthy in Atlantic City (Jamison, 2015).

Marketing expert Seth Godin writes for business, but he is often relevant for the work of school librarians who have "flipped their advocacy switch." The checklist in the sidebar is a periodic review needed to reflect on your ongoing marketing and public relations work that results in a core of advocates who understand that school librarians and school libraries are essential for education of college- and career-ready students.

Question Checklist for Reviewing Your New Marketing Materials

For that new video, or that new brochure, or anything you create that you're hoping will change minds (and spread):

- *What's it for?* When it works, will we be able to tell? What's it supposed to do?
- *Who is it for?* What specific group or tribe or worldview is this designed to resonate with?
- *What does this remind you of?* Who has used this vernacular before? Is it as well done as the previous one was?
- *What's the call to action?* Is there a moment when you are clearly asking people to do something?
- *Show this to ten strangers. Don't say anything. What do they ask you?* Now, ask them what the material is asking them to do.
- *What is the urgency?* Why now?

Your job is not to answer every question; your job is not to close the sale. The purpose of this work is to amplify interest, generate interaction and spread your idea to the people who need to hear it, at the same time that you build trust. (Godin, 2015; used with permission of the author)

CONCLUSION

While the majority of the advocacy work by school librarians is focused on their own library program, it is also important not to ignore the city, state, and federal legislation that matters for school libraries and the profession. Education, intellectual freedom, copyright, open access to research, and many other issues have an impact on students, schools, and school libraries. The old saying that "all politics is local" means that local voices need to join the advocacy offices of state and national library organizations. Thus it is important to join the organizations that speak for libraries, such as the American Library Association, the American Association of School Librarians, your state library organization, and, in some cases, a local or regional organization. Not only is it your professional obligation to move the library profession forward, your dues and participation support their advocacy work and, thus, benefit your students.

The American Library Association's Washington Office creates messaging and has an electronic Legislative Action Center (http://cqrcengage.com/ala/home) to make it quite easy to add your and your core advocates' voices when there is a legislative alert on issues that are important to librarians and libraries. Every state chapter also has the same capability, subsidized in large part by ALA. Through organization electronic mailing lists or even the mobile app from the ALA Washington Office, it takes minimal effort to add your voice to others in the profession. Each voice makes a difference.

The American Library Association's Office of Advocacy's "Advocacy University" (http://www.ala.org/advocacy/advocacy-university) is a portal of resources and messaging that can take marketing and promotion from good to great. Included are very useful resources available for download such as the *Library Advocates Handbook* with tips on how to deal with legislators and the media and techniques for PR. The downloadable "Quotable Facts about America's Libraries" is the size of a business card and contains sound bites about libraries in general and all library types. Quotes such as "Students make 1.3 billion visits to school libraries during the school year, the same as attendance made to movie theaters in 2011 or three times as many visits to national parks" can help when talking to decision makers—or students (ALA, 2012).

> The resources cited in this chapter and more are available in the author's advocacy wiki: http://frugalschoollibrarian.wikispaces.com/. It is possible to join the wiki and be an active participant in advocacy for school librarians and school library programs.

A strong, active marketing plan results in the previously mentioned core of library advocates. As library legislative issues need action, the electronic legislative action centers make it easy to request participation by your library champions via e-mail, Facebook, or Twitter, or a notice on your school library webpage. It's even possible to set up your own "Legislative Action Center" by having a computer open to the ALA Washington Office or your state's action page to make it easy for students, staff, and teachers coming into the school library to add their voices for library legislative action.

Promotion + Marketing = Action, the "offensive" formula mentioned earlier, can result in action when local school library positions are threatened, state education and library funding needs support, or federal legislation for freedom of speech or educational reform is on the docket. Development of a marketing plan takes time, reflection, and action, but it is a professional activity that makes a school library program collaborative with the entire school community from students to local business people.

"Flipping the switch" for advocacy changes your outlook—and changes students' lives.

Suggested School Library Advocacy and Marketing Resources

Activism and the School Library. 2012. ABC-CLIO. Practical tips from successful school library advocates; covers community and legislative advocacy strategies.

Building Influence for the School Librarian: Tenets, Targets and Tactics, 2nd ed. 2003. Linworth. Dr. Gary Hartzell gives insight into the perceptions of school librarians by administrators and teachers—and how to turn them around.

The Indispensable Librarian: Surviving and Thriving in School Libraries in the Information Age, 2nd ed. 2013. Linworth. Doug Johnson's chapter, "Communications and Advocacy," looks at the audiences for school library advocacy and strategies for communication, and gives five practical rules for effective advocacy.

New on the Job: A School Librarian's Guide to Success, 2nd ed. 2015. ALA. Hilda Weisburg's chapter, "Advocacy and You," provides a focus on advocacy, marketing, and public relations both for new people in the school library field and veterans.

The New York City School Library System Handbook, "Section 1: Vision, Mission, Goals, and Expectations," http://schools.nycenet.edu/offices/teachlearn/sls/ Handbook_Section1_VisionMissionGoalsExpectations.pdf. The first steps of a marketing plan.

School Library Monthly, http://www.schoollibrarymonthly.com/articles/index.html. A series of articles on advocacy by Debra Kachel and Christie Kaaland. They and Deborah Levitov are beginning a promising advocacy website, http://school libraryadvocacy.org.

REFERENCES

AASL (American Association of School Librarians). 2009. *Empowering Learners : Guidelines for School Library Media Programs* . Chicago: American Library Association.

———. 2014. "AASL Transforms Learning with New Mission Statement and Strategic Plan." American Library Association. http://www.ala.org/news/press-releases/2014/07/aasl-transforms-learning-new-mission-statement-and-strategic-plan.

———. 2015. "What Is Advocacy?" http://www.ala.org/aasl/advocacy/definitions.

ALA (American Library Association). 2003. *Toolkit for School Library Media Programs: Messages, Ideas, and Strategies for Promoting the Value of Our Libraries and Librarians in the 21st Century*. Chicago: American Library Association and American Association of School Librarians.

———. 2010a. "Campaign for America's Libraries." http://www.ala.org/advocacy/advleg/publicawareness/campaign@yourlibrary/.

———. 2010b. "Frontline Advocacy Toolkit." http://www.ala.org/advocacy/advleg/advocacyuniversity/frontline_advocacy.

———. 2012. "Quotable Facts about America's Libraries." http://www.ala.org/advocacy/advocacy-university.

———. 2013. "Declaration for the Right to School Libraries." http://www.ala.org/advocacy/declaration-right-school-libraries-text-only.

ALSC (Association for Library Service to Children). 2014. "Using Electronic Media." http://www.ala.org/everyday-advocacy/speak-out/electronic-media.

Atlantic City High School. 2014. "Library Policies." http://achs.acboe.org/resources/library-policies.

Buerkett, Rebecca. 2015. Interview by the author. February 7.

Collins, Jim. 2001. *Good to Great*. New York: HarperCollins.

DelGuidice, Margaux, and Rose Luna. 2012. *Make a Big Impact at Your School Board Meeting*. Santa Barbara, CA: Linworth.

Flowers, Rebecca. 2015. E-mail message to the author. February 21.

Godin, Seth. 2015. "Question Checklist for Reviewing Your New Marketing Materials . . ." *Seth's Blog*, January 17. http://sethgodin.typepad.com/seths_blog/2015/01/question-checklist-for-reviewing-your-new-marketing-materials.html.

Haughey, Duncan. 2014. "SMART Goals." *Project SMART*. http://www.projectsmart.co.uk/smart-goals.php.

Jamison, Jennifer. 2015. E-mail message to the author. February 24.

Johns, Sara Kelly. 2008. "What Can Teacher-Librarians Do to Promote Their Work and the School Library Media Program? Offensive Formula: P+M=A." *Teacher Librarian* 36, no. 2: 36–37.

Kowalski, Sue. 2015. "Action and Impact for a School Librarian." E-mail message to the author. February 21.

LaGarde, Jennifer. 2013a. Interview by the author. Telephone. November 13.

———. 2013b. "Joyce's Story: The Ending Is Up to You." *Library Girl*, December 21. http://www.librarygirl.net/2013/12/joyces-story-ending-is-up-to-you.html.

Luther, Stacey. 2015. "Library Mission/Library Vision." Lee High School Media Center. http://www.leehighlibrary.com/mission--vision.html.

Malespina, Elissa. 2015. "Marketing Your Library." http://www.elissamalespina.com/marketing-your-library---keynote.html.

Pine Grove Middle School Library Home Page. 2015. East Syracuse Minoa Central School District. http://pinegrove.libguides.com/home?hs=a.

St. Laurent, Katharine. 2015. Personal Facebook message to author. February 21.

Stripling, Barbara K. 2014. "Reimagining Advocacy for School Libraries." *American Libraries: School Libraries Transform Learning* (September/October Digital Supplement on School Libraries): 6–14. http://edition.pagesuite-professional.co.uk/Launch.aspx?EID=6c7cb940-d8fb-43d8-8ad8-864bf0e83f38.

Valenza, Joyce Kasman. 2004. "Library Website Organizer." In *Power Tools Recharged: 125+ Essential Forms and Presentations for Your School Library Information Program*, 1-26A-1-26B. Chicago: ALA.

Index

About the Editors and the Contributors

Jeannie Allen is the marketing manager at Kitsap Regional Library in Bremerton, Washington. She earned her BA in fine art and graphic design. Jeannie is currently leading her library system through an exciting rebranding effort set to launch to the public in April 2015. The experiences she gained in the competitive, high-pressure fields of retail, real estate, and mortgage banking sales and marketing give her an edge that is needed as she looks for creative and innovative ways to help libraries redefine the way they are viewed today. In her two years with the library, her teams' marketing efforts have been rewarded with a *Library Journal* LibraryAware Community Award, as well as the prestigious American Library Association John Cotton Dana Award.

Brent Bloechle is the library manager of the Maribelle M. Davis Library in Plano, Texas, and has worked at the Plano Public Library System for the past decade. Prior to this, he served as an academic librarian in the Cox School of Business Information Center at Southern Methodist University and as a market researcher for the Dallas/Fort Worth International Airport. Brent earned his MLIS from Texas Woman's University. He recently spoke at Internet Librarian 2013 on "Engaging Your Community with Social Media" and at the 2014 Public Library Association's annual conference on "Meeting Public Service Expectations by Breaking the Service Model." His current responsibilities include systemwide library technology implementation and managing the library system's social media presence.

Heather A. Dalal is an assistant professor/emerging technologies librarian at Rider University. She has an MEd in instructional design and an MLIS. Heather has always been concerned with how students perceive the library and so she focuses her efforts on the promotion and marketing of library tools and services. Heather's other research interests are instructional design, undergraduate research behavior, instructional technologies, and assessment of online training. Heather serves on the Association of College & Research Libraries (ACRL) Distance Learning Section (DLS) Instruction Section, ACRL DLS Standards Committee, the New Jersey Library Association (NJLA) Emerging Technologies Section, the NJLA College and University Section's User Education Committee, and the New Jersey Virtual Academic Library Environment's Shared Information Literacy Committee.

Matthew Daley is the webmaster and graphic designer at the University of Florida Health Science Center Library. He holds an MLIS from Florida State University.

Mary E. Edwards is the distance learning and liaison librarian at the University of Florida Health Science Center Library, where she has worked since 2004. Mary holds a master's degree from the University of South Florida (2003) in library and information science, and in 2011 she earned a doctorate (EdD) in educational technology from the University of Florida.

Jessica Ford is the public relations coordinator for Mid-Continent Public Library, located in Kansas City, Missouri. After receiving her BA in communications from the University of Missouri–Kansas City, Jessica went on to pursue her love of information by attaining her Master of Library Science and Information Technology degree from the University of Missouri–Columbia. After working for years in a branch library, she is now able to combine her communications background with a practical knowledge of the library environment.

Letha Kay Goger is communications librarian at the University of California, Merced Library. She was previously digital librarian for the Institute for the Study of Knowledge Management in Education (ISKME), a nonprofit research institute that focuses on building open knowledge networks, research-based innovation in education, and practice in the use of open educational resources (OER) around the world. In 2009, Letha earned an MA in world cultures and history from the University of California, Merced, with a focus on humanities computing, open knowledge society, and digital libraries. In 2013, she earned her MLIS from San Jose State University and focused her work there on global librarianship and digital libraries.

Paris Hannon is a psychology major at Rider University with an expected graduation date of May 2015. She is a library assistant at the Rider University Moore Library, a position she has held since 2011. She has served in many roles in the library, including print station monitor, reference student help, and circulation staff assistant. Most recently, she is the technological assistant for the emerging technologies librarian, where she is focused on the promotion and marketing of library tools and services and the creation of digital learning objects. Paris has appeared in several of the libraries' award-winning promotional videos. Paris serves as a member of Rider University's Psychology Club, and she also is the creator and designer of her own online thrift shop (http://parislately.bigcartel.com).

Jamie Hazlitt has been a librarian at Loyola Marymount University (LMU) since 2005. As the library's outreach and communications librarian, she synthesizes her skills as a librarian, writer, designer, community organizer, curator, matchmaker, and reluctant tweeter and enthusiastic Instagrammer in order to further the William H. Hannon Library's mission of serving as the cultural and intellectual hub of the LMU campus. She has a BFA in visual communication from the University of Washington and received her MLIS in 2005 from the University of California, Los Angeles. She is the editor and art director of the William H. Hannon Library's award-winning newsletter *Happenings @ Hannon* and has been the recipient of multiple ALA PRXchange Best of Show recognitions for excellence in library publications.

Sara Kelly Johns, a longtime school librarian, is currently an online instructor for Mansfield University's "School Library and Information Technologies" course and was an adjunct professor for the "Library Research Methods through Technology" course at SUNY Plattsburgh from 1990 to 2006. Johns was the president of the New York Library Association (NYLA) for 2013–2014 and is a past president of the American Association of School Librarians (AASL) and the School Library Section of NYLA. She is a current member of the New York State Regents Advisory Committee on Libraries, the American Library Association (ALA) Executive Board, the ALA Literacy Committee, and the ALA Conference Committee, and has served on the ALA Advocacy Committee and the ALA Committee on Legislation Grassroots Subcommittee. Johns has written and presented nationally on school librarians and advocacy.

Robert J. Lackie, MLIS, MA, is professor-librarian and department chairperson for the Franklin F. Moore Library of Rider University. A frequent presenter at library, education, and technology conferences and meetings and published within various professional and scholarly works, Prof. Lackie has also co-written or co-edited three books, the latest entitled *Identity Theft: What You Need to Know* (Amazon Digital Services, 2014). For his teaching, writing, leadership, and service to the library profession, he has received several accolades, including the NJLA 2014 Public Relations Award—Tech

Shoutout Category, the ACRL/New Jersey Chapter 2011 Distinguished Service Award, and the ALA 2006 Ken Haycock Award for Promoting Librarianship, among others. For more details on Professor Lackie's publications, presentations, honors, or other information, please visit his directory page: http://www.rider.edu/faculty/robert-j-lackie.

Bonnie Lafazan is the director of the Woodbridge Campus Library at Berkeley College. She received her MLS from Pratt Institute in 2007 and her JD from New England School of Law in 1996. Ms. Lafazan's current focus is designing creative library programming, developing new marketing and outreach methods for community engagement, and utilizing the latest technologies in order to teach students in the academic environment information literacy, lifelong learning, and digital skills.

Lynn D. Lampert is the interim associate dean at California State University, Northridge, Oviatt Library. Prior to this role, Lynn served as the chair of research, instruction, and outreach services (since 2005) and coordinator of information literacy and instruction (since 2001) at the Oviatt Library. Lynn served as a key member of the Oviatt Library's Learning Commons Planning Team, which managed the two-and-a-half-million-dollar Learning Commons renovation project. Lynn earned both her Master of Arts degree in history and her Master of Library and Information Science from the University of California, Los Angeles. Prior to joining the faculty at the Oviatt Library in 2001, Lynn worked as an information specialist at California Lutheran University.

Coleen Meyers-Martin is coordinator of outreach services at California State University, Northridge, Oviatt Library. She received her MA in library and information science from California State University, San Jose. For the last six years she has overseen many of the library's outreach efforts. During 2013, she coordinated the multifaceted, nearly twenty-thousand-dollar marketing campaign that promoted the Library's Learning Commons renovation project to students, faculty, staff, and community members.

Heather Nicholson is the adult services librarian at Strathcona County Public Library in Sherwood Park, Alberta (Canada). Heather worked in international student exchanges, in workplace wellness, as a junior high school teacher, and as an intern academic librarian before completing her MLIS degree at the University of Western Ontario in April 2011. She managed and marketed the Coaldale Public Library from September 2011 until March 2015.

Hannah F. Norton is a reference and liaison librarian at the University of Florida Health Science Center Library, serving primarily as liaison to the College of Veterinary Medicine, the Department of Medicine, and the College of Medicine Class of 2015. Hannah holds an MS in information studies from the University of Texas at Austin.

Amanda Piekart is the information literacy instructional designer at Berkeley College. She earned her MSLIS from the Pratt Institute in 2009 and is currently pursuing an MS in instructional design and technology. She has previously presented at conferences and webinars that focus on library programming, faculty training, and using LibGuides to create an internal newsletter to promote collaboration within the library.

Jim Staley is the marketing and communications director at Mid-Continent Public Library in Kansas City, Missouri. He has degrees in advertising and public administration. As the first marketing director for the three-county library system, Jim was responsible for developing a systemwide approach to focused, patron-centered marketing. In his eight years at the library, his department has concentrated on providing marketing support that emphasizes the cultivation of appropriate service offerings, adaptation of new technology, and a brand that expands the community's view of what the library offers. Mid-Continent Public Library won a 2013 John Cotton Dana Award for its Access branding campaign and the 2014 IMLS National Medal for Library Service. Before coming to MCPL, Jim worked as both a nonprofit do-gooder and an advertising agency stooge.

Nina C. Stoyan-Rosenzweig is the founding archivist and historian for the University of Florida Health Science Center Libraries and J. Hillis Miller Health Science Center. Her background includes graduate work at the University of Pennsylvania and University of Michigan. Her work includes running the Health Science Center archives, developing exhibits, and teaching on the history of medicine.

Michele R. Tennant is the assistant director of the Health Science Center Library, heading the Biomedical and Health Information Services Department, and bioinformatics librarian for the Genetics Institute at the University of Florida. Michele received her PhD in biology from Wayne State University and her MLIS from the University of California, Los Angeles.

Erica Thorsen is a librarian at Albemarle High School in Charlottesville, Virginia. Erica attended Pace University and achieved a BA in English, then went on to CUNY, Queens College, for her MLS. Working as a public librarian in Port Chester, New York, Erica continued in Pace University's

,ducational Technology graduate program. Once certified as a library media specialist, Erica worked at the high school level in both Pleasantville and Syosset, New York. Erica moved and changed levels, working at Polk Elementary School in Dearborn Heights, Michigan, and attended Wayne State University's instructional technology graduate program. Returning to librarianship, Erica obtained a position at Meriwether Lewis Elementary School in Charlottesville, Virginia. After four years there, Erica wanted to return to the high school level and transferred to Albemarle High School.

M. Sandra Wood, MLS, MBA, is librarian emerita at Penn State University Libraries and a fellow of the Medical Library Association. Ms. Wood is founding and current editor of *Medical Reference Services Quarterly* (in its thirty-fourth volume). She was a librarian for over thirty-five years at the George T. Harrell Library, Milton S. Hershey Medical Center, Pennsylvania State University, specializing in reference, education, and database services. Ms. Wood has written or edited more than twelve books, the latest two entitled *Health Sciences Librarianship* and *Successful Library Fundraising: Best Practices* (both with Rowman & Littlefield Publishers, 2014).